The Philosophy of
Spiritual Activity

The Philosophy of Spiritual Activity

BASIC FEATURES OF A MODERN WORLD VIEW

Results of Soul Observation
Arrived at by the Scientific Method

Rudolf Steiner

Anthroposophic Press

This volume is a translation of *Die Philosophie der Freiheit*. The German volume is number four in the Collected Edition of Rudolf Steiner's works. It was translated by William Lindeman.

© 1986 by Anthroposophic Press

Library of Congress Cataloging-in-Publication Data

Steiner, Rudolf, 1861–1925.
    The philosophy of spiritual activity.

    Translation of: Die Philosophie der Freiheit.
    Bibliography: p.
    1. Anthroposophy. I. Lindeman, William. II. Title.
BP595.S894P4613 1986   299'.935   86-1246
ISBN: 0-88010-157-1
        0-88010-156-3 (pbk.)

10 9 8 7 6 5 4 3 2

Cover: Graphic form by Rudolf Steiner
(originally as a study for the
book *Truth and Science*)
Layout and lettering, Peter Stebbing

Printed in the United States of America

Contents

Preface to the Revised Edition, 1918

Everything to be discussed in this book is oriented toward two root questions of human soul life. One question is whether a possibility exists of viewing the being of man in such a way that this view proves to be a support for everything else which, through experience and science, approaches him but which he feels cannot support itself and can be driven by doubt and critical judgment into the realm of uncertainty. The other question is this: Is man, as a being who wants and wills, justified in considering himself to be free, or is this inner freedom a mere illusion that arises in him because he does not see the threads of necessity upon which his willing depends just as much as any happening in nature? No artificial spinning out of thoughts calls forth this question. It comes before the soul quite naturally in a particular disposition of the soul. And one can feel that the soul would lack something of what it should be if it never once saw itself placed, with a greatest possible earnestness in questioning, before the two possibilities: freedom or necessity of the will. It is to be shown in this book that the soul-experiences which the human being has to undergo through the second question depend upon which point of view he is able to take with regard to the first. The attempt is made to show that there is a view of the being of man which can support his other knowledge; and furthermore, to indicate that with this view a full justification is won for the idea of the freedom of the will, if only the soul region is first found in which free willing can unfold itself.

The view under discussion here with respect to both these questions presents itself as one which, once gained, can itself become a part of active soul life. A theoretical answer is not given which, once acquired, merely carries with it a conviction preserved by memory. For the way of picturing things which underlies this book, such an answer would be only a seeming one. No such fixed and final answer is given, but rather a region of experience of the soul is indicated, in which, through the inner activity of the soul itself, the question is answered anew in a living way at any moment that the human being needs it. For someone who has once found the region of the soul in which these questions evolve, the real view of this region gives just what he needs for both these riddles of life; then, with what he has achieved, he can travel on into the distances and depths of this enigmatical life as his need and destiny move him.—With this, a knowledge seems to be indicated which, through its own life and through the relatedness of its own life to the whole human soul life, proves its justification and worth.

This is how I thought about the content of this book

as I wrote it down twenty-five years ago. Today also I must write such sentences when I want to characterize the thoughts toward which this book aims. I limited myself as I wrote at that time, not to say *more* than what is connected in the *closest sense* to the two root questions characterized above. If someone should be surprised about the fact that he does not yet find in this book any allusion to the region of the world of spiritual experience that is described by me in later books, I would ask him to bear in mind that at that time I did not want, in fact, to give a description of the results of spiritual research, but wanted rather first to build the foundation upon which such results can rest. This *Philosophy of Spiritual Activity* contains no such specialized results, just as little as it contains specialized natural–scientific results; but what it does contain is indispensable, in my opinion, to anyone who is striving for certainty in such knowledge. What is said in the book can also be acceptable to those who, for one or another reason which is valid for them, want to have nothing to do with the results of my spiritual-scientific research. But what is attempted here can also be of importance for a person who can regard these spiritual-scientific results as something to which he is drawn. It is this: to show how an unbiased consideration, extending solely to these two questions which lay the foundation for *all* knowing activity, leads to the view that the human being lives in the midst of a true spiritual world. What is striven for in this book is to justify a knowledge of the spiritual realm *before* entry into spiritual experience. And this justification is undertaken in such a way that one needs nowhere at all in these expositions to cast a sidelong glance at the experiences put forward by me later, in order to find what is said here acceptable, if one can or wants to enter into the nature of these expositions themselves.

So this book seems to me on the one hand then to occupy a position completely separate from my actual spiritual-scientific writings, and yet on the other hand to be most closely bound up with them also. All this has moved me now, after twenty-five years, to republish the content of the book in a virtually unchanged form. I have only made some additions to a number of chapters. The experiences I have had with people's misconceptions about what I had written made such detailed amplifications seem necessary to me. I have only made changes where what I wanted to say a quarter of a century ago seems to me today to be awkwardly expressed. (Only someone with ill will could possibly be moved by these changes to say that I have changed my basic conviction.)

The book has been out of print for many years already. Although it seems to me, as is apparent from what has just been said, that what I expressed twenty-five years ago about the two questions should still be expressed in the same way today, I hesitated for a long time to prepare this new edition. I asked myself again and again whether, in this or that passage, I did not have to come to terms with the numerous philosophical views that have come to light since the appearance of the first edition. The demands of my purely spiritual-scientific research lately have prevented me from doing this in the way I would want. But now, after the most thorough possible survey of current philosophical work, I have convinced myself that, as tempting as such a task would be in itself, it is not something to be taken up in the context of what is meant to be said through my book. What seemed to me necessary to be said about more recent philosophical directions from the point of view taken in the *Philosophy of Spiritual Activity*, may be found in the second volume of my *Riddles of Philosophy*.

April 1918   Rudolf Steiner

SCIENCE OF
SPIRITUAL ACTIVITY (*FREIHEIT*)⋆

⋆*Wissenchaft der Freiheit.* See Translator's Appendix with reference to
translation of *Freiheit* as *spiritual activity.*

I
Conscious Human Action

Is man,* in his thinking and doing, a spiritually *free* being, or does he stand under the compulsion of an iron necessity of purely natural lawfulness? Upon few questions has so much keen thought been focused as upon this one. The idea of the freedom of human will has found warm adherents as well as stubborn opponents in great number. There are people who, in their moral fervor, pronounce anyone narrow-minded who can deny so evident a *fact* as inner freedom. These are opposed by others who see it as eminently unscientific for someone to believe that the lawfulness of nature is interrupted in the sphere of human action and thinking. One and the same thing is here pronounced just as often to be the most prized possession of mankind as it is to be the worst illusion. Endless ingenuity has been expended to explain how human

*Since English has not yet produced a neutral word for what we are (even "human being" has the word "man" in it), one must still ask the reader to remove any connotations of gender from such words.
—Translator's note.

freedom can be compatible with the working of nature, to which, after all, man also belongs. No less pains have been taken from another side to attempt to make comprehensible how such a delusion could have arisen. That we have here to do with one of the most important questions of life, of religion, of praxis, and of science—this anyone feels in whom the opposite of thoroughness is not the most outstanding feature of his character. And it is one of the sad indications of the superficiality of contemporary thinking that a book, which wants to formulate from the results of recent research into nature a "new belief" (David Friedrich Strauss, *The New and the Old Belief**), contains nothing about this question except the words: "We do not have to go into the question here of the freedom of human will. The supposedly neutral freedom of choice has always been recognized as an empty specter by every philosophy worthy of the name; the moral evaluation of human actions and attitudes, however, remains untouched by that question." I do not quote this passage here because I believe that the book in which it stands has particular significance, but rather because it seems to me to express the opinion to which the majority of our thinking contemporaries is able to raise itself with respect to the matter in question. Everyone who claims to have outgrown his scientific childhood seems to know today that being free could not consist in choosing, wholly at will, one or the other of two possible actions. There is always, it is declared, a very definite *reason* why a person carries out just one particular action from a number of possible ones.

*Der alte und neue Glaube

That seems obvious. Nevertheless, right to the present day, the main attacks of the opponents of freedom direct themselves only against freedom of choice. Herbert Spencer for one, who lives in opinions that are becoming more widespread with each day, says in his *Principles of Psychology**: "*But that every one is at liberty to desire or not to desire*, which is the real proposition involved in the dogma of free will, is negated as much by the internal perception of every one as by the contents of the preceding chapters." Others also start from the same point of view in combating the concept of free will. In germinal form all the expositions relating to this are to be found already in Spinoza. His clear and simple argument against the idea of freedom has been repeated innumerable times since then, but cloaked, for the most part, in the most hairsplitting theoretical doctrines, so that it becomes difficult to discern the plain thought process which alone matters. Spinoza writes in a letter of October or November 1674: "I call a thing *free*, namely, which exists and acts out of the pure necessity of its nature, and I call a thing *compelled* which is determined in its existing and working by something else in a definite and fixed way. So, for example, God exists, although with necessity, still freely, because he exists out of the necessity of his nature alone. In the same way, God knows himself and everything else freely, because it follows out of the necessity of his nature alone that he knows everything. You see, therefore, that I place freedom not in a free decision but rather in a free necessity."

"But let us come down to created things which are all

*Part IV, Chap. IX, par. 207.

of them determined by outer causes to exist and work in a fixed and definite way. In order to see this more distinctly let us picture to ourselves something completely simple. Let us say a stone, for example, receives from an external cause propelling it, a certain quantity of motion with which afterward, when the impact of the external cause has ceased, the stone necessarily continues to move itself along. This perseverance of the stone in its motion is compelled and not necessary, because it must be defined through the impact of an external cause. What here holds good for the stone, holds good for every other single thing, no matter how complex and versatile it may be, namely, that everything is determined with necessity by an external cause to exist and work in a fixed and definite way.''

''*Please suppose now that the stone, while moving along, is thinking, and knows that it is striving as hard as it can to continue in motion. This stone, which is only conscious of its striving and is not at all indifferent to what it is doing, will believe that it is completely free and that it is continuing in its motion for no other reason than because it wants to. This, however, is that human freedom which everyone claims to possess and which consists only in the fact that people are conscious of their desires, but do not know the causes by which people are determined.* Thus the child believes that it is free in desiring milk, and the angry boy is free in demanding revenge, and the coward free in his flight. Furthermore, the drunken person believes it to be his free decision to say now what he would rather not have said when sober again; and since this biased view is innate to all people, one cannot easily free oneself from it. For although experience teaches us well enough that people are the least able to moderate their desires and that, when moved by two opposing passions, they see the better and do the worse, even so they consider themselves free, because in fact they do desire many things less strongly and many a desire can easily be restrained by the memory of some other preoccupation of theirs.''

Because an opinion is here put forward that is clearly and definitely expressed, it is also easy to uncover the basic error that lies within it. One supposes that man carries out an action, when driven to it by some reason or other, with the same necessity as a stone carries out a definite motion after an impact. Only because man has a consciousness of his action does he consider himself to be the free originator of it. In doing so he overlooks, however, the fact that a cause is driving him which he must follow absolutely. The error in this thought process is soon discovered. Spinoza, and all who think like him, overlook the fact that man does not only have a consciousness of his action, but can also have a consciousness of the causes by which he is led. No one will dispute the fact that the child is *unfree* when it desires milk, that the drunken person is so, when he says things which he later regrets. Both know nothing of the causes that are active in the depths of their organism and under whose irresistible compulsion they stand. But is it right to lump together actions of this kind with those in which man is conscious not only of his action, but also of the reasons which move him? Are the actions of men of one and the same kind then? May the act of the soldier on the battlefield, that of the scientific researcher in his laboratory, of the statesman in complex diplomatic affairs be placed scientifically on the same level with that of a child when it desires milk? Certainly it is true that it is best to attempt the solution of a problem where the matter is at its simplest. But the lack of ability to make distinctions has often caused endless confusion. And it is after all a far-reaching difference whether I know why I do something, or whether that is not the case. At first sight this seems to be an entirely obvious truth. And yet it is never asked by the opponents of freedom whether, then, a stimulus to action which I know and understand signifies for me a compulsion in the same sense as the organic process which causes the child to cry for milk.

Eduard von Hartmann maintains in his *Phenomenology of Moral Consciousness** that human willing depends upon two main factors: upon the stimulus to action and upon one's character. If one looks upon human beings as all identical or at least upon their differences as negligible, then their willing appears as though determined from *outside*, that is, by the circumstances that come to meet them. If one considers, however, that different people make a mental picture into a stimulus to action only if their character is such that it is moved by the corresponding mental picture to desire something, then the human being appears to be determined from *within* and not from *without*. Because he now, according to his character, must first make a mental image forced upon him from outside into a stimulus for action, the person believes that he is free, that is, independent of outer stimuli to action.

**Phaenomenologie des sittlichen Bewusstseins*

The truth however is, according to Eduard von Hartmann, that: "Even if we ourselves, however, must first raise mental pictures into motives, still we do not do this arbitrarily, but rather according to the necessity of our characterological disposition, *therefore anything but freely."* Here also no attention is paid to the difference that exists between stimuli to action which I first let work upon me after I have permeated them with my consciousness, and those which I follow without possessing a clear knowledge of them.

And this leads us directly to the standpoint from which the subject is to be considered here. May the question of the freedom of our will be asked at all by itself, in a one-sided way? And if not: with what other question must it necessarily be linked?

If there is a difference between a conscious stimulus to my action and an unconscious urge to it, then the first will also bring with it an action that must be judged differently than one out of blind impulse. The question as to this difference will therefore be the first. And what this question yields will then determine what position we have to take with respect to the actual question of inner freedom itself.

What does it mean to *know* the reasons for one's action? One has given this question too little attention, because unfortunately one has always torn into two parts what is an inseparable whole: the human being. One differentiated between the doer and the knower, and only the one who matters the most was left out: the one who acts out of knowledge.

One says that man is free when he stands only under

the dominion of his reason and not under that of his animal desires, or that inner freedom means to be able to determine one's life and action according to purposes and decisions.

Absolutely nothing is gained by assertions of this kind, however. For that is in fact the question, whether reason, whether purposes and decisions, exercise a compulsion on the human being in the same way animal desires do. If without my cooperation a rational decision rises up in me with exactly the same necessity as hunger and thirst, then I can only follow it by necessity, and my inner freedom is an illusion.

Another form of expression runs: To be free does not mean to be able to want what one wants to, but rather, to be able to do what one wants to. The poet-philosopher Robert Hamerling has characterized this thought in sharply outlined words in his *Atomistic Theory of Will*★: "The human being can, to be sure, *do* what he wants to— but he cannot *want* what he wants to, because his wanting is determined by *motives*!—He cannot want what he wants to? But let us consider these words again more closely. Is there a reasonable sense in them? Freedom of will would therefore have to consist in the fact that one could want something without reason, without motive? But what then does wanting mean other than *having a reason* for preferring to do, or to strive after, this rather than that? To want something without reason, without motive, would mean to want something, *without wanting it*. With the concept of wanting, the concept of motive is *inseparably*

★*Atomistik des Willens*

linked. Without a determining motive the will is an empty *capability*: only through the motive does it become active and real. It is therefore entirely correct that the human will is not "free" inasmuch as its direction is always determined by the strongest of its motives. But it must on the other hand be admitted that it is absurd, in the face of this "unfreedom," to speak of a conceivable "freedom" of the will which would end up being able to want what one does *not* want."

Here also, only motives in general are discussed, without taking into consideration the difference between unconscious and conscious ones. If a motive works upon me and I am compelled to follow it because it proves itself to be the "strongest" of its kind, then thinking about inner freedom ceases to make any sense. How should it be of any significance for me whether I can do something or not, if I am *compelled* by the motive to do it? The point here is not whether, when the motive has worked upon me, I can then do something or not, but rather whether there are only such motives that work with compelling necessity. If I *must* want something, then, under certain circumstances, it might be of the greatest indifference to me whether I can also do it. If, because of my character and because of circumstances prevailing in my environment, a motive is forced upon me that to my thinking shows itself to be irrational, then I would even have to be glad if I could not do what I want to.

The main point is not whether I can carry out a decision made, but rather how *the decision arises in me.*

That which distinguishes man from all other organic beings is based on his rational thinking. Activity he has in common with other organisms. Nothing is gained by searching for analogies in the animal kingdom to elucidate the concept of freedom for the actions of human beings. Modern natural science loves such analogies. And when it has succeeded in finding something among animals that is similar to human behavior, it believes it has touched upon the most important question of knowledge about the human being. To what misunderstandings this opinion leads, is shown, for example, in the book *The Illusion of Free Will** by P. Rée, 1885, who says the following about freedom: "That it seems to us as though the motion of the stone were by necessity, and the willing of the donkey were not by necessity, is easily explainable. The causes which move the stone are of course external and visible. The causes, however, by virtue of which the donkey wills, are internal and invisible: between us and the place of their activity the donkey's skull is to be found. . . . One does not see the causal dependence, and supposes therefore that it is not present. The will, one explains, is indeed the cause of the donkey's turning around, but the willing itself is independent; it is an absolute beginning." So here too actions of the human being in which he has a consciousness of the reasons for his action, are again simply passed over, for Rée explains: "Between us and the place of their activity the donkey's skull is to be found." To judge already from these words, —Rée has no inkling of the fact that there are actions not of the donkey, to be sure, but certainly of people—for

---

**Die Illusion der Willensfreiheit*

which the motive *that has become conscious* lies between us
and the action. He also proves this once again a few pages
later through the words: "We do not perceive the *causes*
by which our willing is determined; therefore we suppose
that it is not causally determined at all."

But, enough of examples which prove that many fight
against freedom without knowing at all what freedom is.

It is entirely obvious that an action which the doer
performs, without knowing why he does it, cannot be
free. But how does the matter stand with the kind of action whose reasons are known? This leads us to the question: What is the origin and the significance of thinking?
For without knowledge about the *thinking* activity of the
soul, a concept of knowing about anything, including an
action, is not possible. When we know what thinking in
general signifies, then it will also be easy to become clear
about the role of thinking in human action. "Only with
thinking does the soul, with which the animal is also endowed, first become spirit," says Hegel rightly, and
therefore thinking will also give to human action its characteristic stamp.

This is not to assert by any means that all our action
flows only out of the sober deliberations of our intellect.
To set forth only those actions as in the highest sense
human which issue from abstract judgment, is very far
from my intention. But the moment our action lifts itself
up out of the area of the satisfaction of purely animal
desires, what moves us to act is always intermixed with
thoughts. Love, compassion, patriotism are mainsprings
of action which do not let themselves be reduced into

cold concepts of the intellect. One says: The heart, the *Gemüt**★* come here into their own. Without a doubt. But the heart and the *Gemüt* do not create what it is that moves us to act. They presuppose it and take it into their domain. Within my heart compassion appears when, in my consciousness, the mental picture arises of a person who arouses compassion. The way to the heart is through the head. Even love is no exception to this. When it is not the mere expression of the sex drive, it is then based upon the mental pictures which we make for ourselves of the loved one. And the more idealistic these mental pictures are, the more blissful is the love. Here also the thought is father to the feeling. One says: Love makes us blind to the weaknesses of the loved one. The matter can also be grasped the other way round and it can be maintained that love opens the eye in fact for precisely the good qualities of the loved one. Many pass these good qualities by without an inkling, without noticing them. One person sees them, and just because he does, love awakens in his soul. What has he done other than make for himself a mental picture of something of which a hundred others have none. They do not have the love because they lack the *mental picture.*

We may grasp the subject however we want: it must become ever clearer that the question about the nature of human action presupposes the other about the origin of thinking. I will turn, therefore, first of all to this question.

★We have no word for *Gemüt* in English. It points more to the totality of man's inner being than "heart" does.—Translator's note.

II
The Fundamental Desire for Knowledge

Two souls alas! are dwelling in my breast;
And each is fain to leave its brother.
The one, fast clinging, to the world adheres
With clutching organs, in love's sturdy lust;
The other strongly lifts itself from dust
To yonder high ancestral spheres.

Faust I, Sc. 2
(Priest translation)

With these words Goethe expresses a characteristic deeply founded in human nature. Man is not whole in the organization of his being. He demands always more than the world gives him of its own accord. Nature has given us needs; among these are such whose satisfaction it has left to our own activity. Abundant are the gifts apportioned us, but still more abundant is our desiring. We seem born to be discontented. One particular instance of this discontent is our urge to know. We look twice at a tree. The one time we see its branches at rest, the other time in motion. We do not content ourselves with this observation. Why does the tree present itself to us the one time at rest, the other time in motion? We ask about things in this

15

way. Every look into nature produces a number of questions in us. With every phenomenon that comes our way a task is set us along with it. Every experience becomes a riddle for us. We see emerge from the egg a being that resembles the mother animal; we ask for the reason for this resemblance. We observe in a living being growth and development to a particular level of perfection; we seek the determining factors of this experience. Nowhere are we content with what nature spreads out before our senses. We seek everywhere what we call *explanation* of the facts.

The fact that what we seek in things exceeds what is directly given us in them, splits our entire being in two parts; we become conscious of our polar opposition to the world. We confront the world as independent beings. The universe appears to us in the polarity: *I* and *world*.

We erect this wall of separation between us and the world as soon as consciousness lights up within us. But never do we lose the feeling that we belong even so to the world, that a bond endures that joins us to it, that we are not beings *outside*, but rather inside the universe.

This feeling creates the striving to bridge the polarity. And the entire spiritual striving of mankind ultimately consists in the bridging of this polarity. The history of our spiritual life is a continuous searching for the unity between us and the world. Religion, art, and science all pursue this goal. The religious believer seeks, within the revelation which God allots to him, the solution to the world riddle that his "I," not content with the world of mere phenomena, poses him. The artist seeks to fashion into matter the ideas of his "I," in order to reconcile what lives in his inner being with the outer world. He too feels himself unsatisfied by the world of mere phenomena and seeks to mold into it that something more which his "I," transcending the world of phenomena, contains. The thinker searches for the laws of phenomena; he strives, thinking, to penetrate what he experiences observing. Only when we have made the *world content* into our *thought content*, only then do we find again the connection from which we ourselves have detached ourselves. We will see later on that this goal will only be attained if the task of the scientific researcher is in fact grasped much more deeply than is often done. The whole relationship I have presented here confronts us in a world-historical manifestation: in the polarity of the one-world view or *monism*, to the two-world theory or *dualism*. Dualism directs its gaze only upon the separation between "I" and world brought about by the consciousness of man. Its whole striving is an ineffectual struggle to reconcile this polarity, which it sometimes calls *spirit* and *matter*, sometimes *subject* and *object*, sometimes *thinking* and *phenomenon*. It has a feeling that there must be a bridge between the two worlds, but it is not capable of finding it. In that the human being experiences himself as "I," he cannot but think of this "I" as being on the side of the *spirit*; and in that he sets the world over against this "I," he must reckon to this world the world of perception given to the senses, the *material* world. Man places himself thereby into the polarity of spirit and matter. He must do this all the more since his own body belongs to the material world. The "I" belongs in this way to the spiritual as a part of it; the *material* things and processes that are perceived by the senses belong to the "world." All the riddles relating to spirit and matter must be found again by man within the fundamental riddle of his own being. *Monism* directs its gaze upon the unity alone and seeks to deny or obliterate the polarities actually present. Neither of the two views can satisfy, for they do not do justice to the facts. Dualism sees spirit ("I") and matter (world) as two fundamentally different entities, and therefore cannot grasp how the two can interact with each other. How should the spirit know what is going on in matter, if matter's essential nature is entirely alien to it? Or how should the spirit under these circumstances work upon matter in such a way that its intentions transform themselves into deeds? The most ingenious and most contradictory hypotheses were set up in order to solve these questions. Up to the present, however, monism is not in a much better position. It has sought help up till now in three ways: either it denies the spirit and becomes materialism; or it denies matter, in order to seek its salvation in spiritualism; or, it maintains that matter and spirit are already inseparably joined even in the most simple entity in the world, for which reason one need not be surprised if these two kinds of existence, which after all are nowhere separated, appear within the human being.

Materialism can never provide a satisfactory explanation of the world. For every attempt at an explanation must begin with one's forming *thoughts* for oneself about the phenomena of the world. Materialism therefore takes its start with the *thought* of matter or of material processes. Thus it already has two different realms of facts before it: the material world and thoughts about it. It seeks to understand the latter by grasping them as a purely material process. It believes that thinking takes place in the brain in about the same way as digestion does in the animal organs. Just as it attributes to matter mechanical and organic effects, so it also ascribes to it the capability, under specific conditions, to think. It forgets that it has now only transferred the problem to another place. It attributes the capability of thinking not to itself but to matter. And in doing so it is back again at its starting point. How does matter come to reflect upon its own being? Why is it not simply satisfied with itself and accepting of its existence? The materialist has turned his gaze away from the specific subject, from our own "I," and has arrived at an indefinite, hazy configuration. And here the same riddle comes to meet him. The materialistic view is not able to solve the problem, but only to shift it.

How do matters stand with the spiritualistic view? The pure *spiritualist* denies matter in its independent existence and apprehends it only as product of the spirit. If he applies this world view to solving the riddle of his own human nature, he is, in doing so, driven into a corner. Confronting the "I," which can be placed on the side of spirit, there stands, without intermediary, the sensory world. Into this, no *spiritual* entry seems to open; this world has to be perceived and experienced by the "I" through material processes. The "I" does not find any such material processes within itself, if it wants to be considered only as a spiritual entity. The sense world is never present in what the "I" works through spiritually for itself. It seems the "I" must admit that the world would remain closed to it, if the "I" were not to put itself into a relationship with it in an unspiritual way. In like manner, when we come to act, we must transform our intentions into reality with the help of the material substances and forces. We are, therefore, reliant on the outer world. The most extreme spiritualist, or if you will, the thinker presenting himself as extreme spiritualist through absolute idealism, is Johann Gottlieb Fichte. He attempted to derive the whole edifice of the world out of the "I." What he has actually achieved thereby is a magnificent *thought picture* of the world, without any content of experience. Just as little as it is possible for the materialist to banish spirit by decree, is it possible for the spiritualist to banish the outer material world by decree.

Because the human being, when he directs his knowledge to the "I," perceives to begin with the working of this "I" within the thinking elaboration of the world of ideas, the spiritualistically oriented world view can feel itself tempted, by looking at its own human nature, to acknowledge of the spirit only this world of ideas. Spiritualism becomes in this way one-sided idealism. It does not come to the point, *through* the world of ideas, of seeking a *spiritual* world; it sees in the world of ideas itself the spiritual world. It is compelled thereby to remain as though spellbound within the activity of the "I" itself.

A curious variant of idealism is the view of Friedrich Albert Lange which he has presented in his widely read *History of Materialism.** He supposes that materialism is totally right when it explains all phenomena, including our thinking, as the product of purely material processes;

---

*Geschichte des Materialismus

but, conversely, matter and its processes themselves are again a product of our thinking. "The senses give us . . . *effects* of things, not accurate pictures, let alone the things themselves. To these mere effects belong however also the senses themselves, along with the brain and the movements of molecules thought to be in it." That means our thinking is produced by the material processes, and these by the thinking of the "I." Lange's philosophy is thereby nothing other than the story, translated into concepts, of the intrepid Münchhausen, who holds himself up freely in the air by his own pigtail.

The third form of monism is that which sees within the simplest entity (atom) the two entities matter and spirit already united. But all that is achieved here is that the question, which actually arises in our consciousness, is shifted to another arena. How does the simple entity come to manifest itself in a twofold way, if it is an undivided whole?

With respect to all these standpoints we must note that the basic and original polarity comes to meet us first of all within our own consciousness. It is we who detach ourselves from the mother ground of nature, and place ourselves as "I" over against the "world." Goethe expresses this classically in his essay "Nature," even though his approach may at first be considered completely unscientific: "We live in the midst of her (nature) and are foreign to her. She speaks unceasingly to us and does not betray her secret." But Goethe also knows the reverse side: "Human beings are all within her and she within all human beings."

As true as it is that we have estranged ourselves from

nature, it is just as true that we feel that we are within it and belong to it. It can only be its own working that also lives in us.

We must find the way back to it again. A simple consideration can show us this way. We have, it is true, torn ourselves from nature; but we must nevertheless have taken something over with us into our own being. We must seek out this being of nature within us, and then we will also find the connection again. Dualism neglects to do this. It considers the inner being of man to be a spiritual entity totally foreign to nature and seeks to attach this entity onto nature. No wonder that it cannot find the connecting link. We can find nature outside us only when we first know it *within* us. What is akin to it in our own inner being will be our guide. Our course is thereby sketched out for us. We do not want to engage in any speculations about the interaction of nature and spirit. We want, however, to descend into the depths of our own being, in order to find there those elements which we have rescued in our flight from nature.

 The exploration of our being must bring us the solution to the riddle. We must come to a point where we can say to ourselves: here we are no longer merely "I," here lies something that is more than "I."

I am prepared for the objection that many who have read this far will not find my expositions to be in conformity with "the present-day position of scholarship." I can only reply that up till now I have not wanted to concern myself with scholarship, but rather with the simple description of what everyone experiences within his own consciousness. Individual sentences about attempts of consciousness to reconcile itself with the world have also been included only in order to make the actual facts clear. I have therefore also not thought it important to use such single expressions as "I," "spirit," "world," "nature," and so forth in the precise way that is usual in psychology and philosophy. Everyday consciousness does not know the sharp distinctions of scholarship, and until now we have merely been dealing with an assimilation of the everyday state of affairs. My concern is not how scholarship has interpreted consciousness until now, but rather how consciousness expresses itself in every moment.

III
Thinking in the Service
of Apprehending the World

When I observe how a billiard ball that is struck communicates its motion to another, I remain thereby completely without influence on the course of this observed occurrence. The direction of motion and the velocity of the second ball are determined by the direction and velocity of the first. As long as I act merely as observer, I can say something about the motion of the second ball only when the motion has occurred. The matter is different when I begin to reflect on the content of my observation. My reflection has the purpose of forming concepts about the occurrence. I bring the concept of an elastic ball into connection with certain other concepts of mechanics, and take into consideration the particular circumstances which prevail in the present case. I seek, that is, to add to the occurrence that runs its course without my participation a second occurrence that takes place in the conceptual sphere. The latter is dependent upon me. This shows itself through the fact that I can content myself with the observation and forgo any seeking for concepts, if I have no need of them. But if this need is present, then I will rest content only when I have brought the concepts ball, elasticity, motion, impact, velocity, etc. into a certain interconnection, to which the observed occurrence stands in a definite relationship. As certain as it is, now, that the occurrence takes place independently of me, it is just as certain that the conceptual process cannot occur without my participation.

Whether this activity of mine really issues from my own independent being, or whether the modern physiologists are right who say that we cannot think as we want, but rather must think as determined by the thoughts and thought connections now present in our consciousness (cf. Ziehen, *Guidelines of Physiological Psychology*★), is a question that will be the subject of a later discussion. For the moment we merely want to establish the fact that, for the objects and occurrences given us without our participation, we feel ourselves constantly compelled to seek concepts and conceptual connections that stand in a certain relationship to what is given. Whether the activity is in truth *our* activity, or whether we perform it according to an unalterable necessity, this question we will leave aside for the moment. That this activity appears to us at first as our own is without question. We know full well that along with objects, their concepts are not given us at the same time. That I myself am the active one may rest on an illusion; to immediate observation, in any case, the

---

★*Leitfaden der physiologischen Psychologie*

matter presents itself that way. The question is now: What do we gain through the fact that we find a conceptual counterpart to an occurrence?

There is for me a far-reaching difference between the way that the parts of an occurrence interact with each other before and after the discovery of the corresponding concepts. Mere observation can follow the parts of a given occurrence in progress; their connection, however, before recourse is taken to concepts, remains dark. I see the first billiard ball move toward the second in a certain direction and with a definite velocity; what will happen after the resulting impact, this I must wait for, and then again I also can only follow it with my eyes. Let us suppose that, at the moment of impact, someone covered the field on which the occurrence takes place; then I—as mere observer—am without knowledge of what happens afterwards. It is different if, for the constellation of relationships, I have found the corresponding concepts before the covering takes place. In this case I can say what will happen, even if the possibility of observation ceases. An occurrence or object that is merely observed does not of itself reveal anything about its connection with other occurrences or objects. This connection becomes visible only when observation joins itself with thinking.

Observation and thinking are the two starting points for all the spiritual striving of man, insofar as he is conscious of such a striving. The workings of common sense and the most intricate scientific research rest on these two basic pillars of our spirit. The philosophers have started from various ultimate polarities: idea and reality, subject and object, phenomenon and thing-in-itself, "I" and not-"I," idea and will, concept and matter, force and substance, conscious and unconscious. It is easily shown, however, that the polarity of *observation* and *thinking* must precede all these others as the most important for the human being.

Whatever principle we may ever set up: we must show that it was somewhere observed by us, or express it in the form of a clear thought which can also be thought by everyone else. Every philosopher who begins to speak about his ultimate principles must make use of the conceptual form, and thereby of thinking. By doing so he admits indirectly that he already presupposes thinking as part of his activity. Whether thinking or something else is the main element of world evolution, about this nothing yet is determined here. But that the philosopher, without thinking, can gain no knowledge of world evolution, this is clear from the start. In the coming into being of world phenomena, thinking may play a secondary role; but in the coming into being of a view about them, a main role certainly does belong to thinking.

Now with respect to observation, it lies in the nature of our organization that we need it. Our thinking about a horse and the object "horse" are two things which for us appear separately. And this object is accessible to us only through observation. As little as we are able, by mere staring at a horse, to make a concept of it for ourselves, just as little are we capable, by mere thinking, to bring forth a corresponding object.

In sequence of time, observation comes in fact before thinking. For even thinking we must learn to know first through observation. It was essentially the description of an observation when we gave an account at the beginning of this chapter of how thinking is kindled by an occurrence but goes beyond what is thus given before our thinking participation. It is through observation that we first become aware of everything that enters the circle of our experiences. The content of sensations, of perceptions, of contemplations, our feelings, acts of will, dream and fantasy images, mental pictures, concepts and ideas, all illusions and hallucinations, are given to us through *observation*.

But as object of observation, thinking differs essentially from all other things. The observation of a table or of a tree occurs for me as soon as these objects arise on the horizon of my experiences. My thinking about these objects, however, I do not observe at the same time. I observe the table, I carry out my thinking about the table, but I do not observe my thinking at the same moment. I must first transfer myself to a standpoint outside of my own activity, if I want, besides the table, to observe also my thinking about the table. Whereas the observing of objects and occurrences, and the thinking about them, are the entirely commonplace state of affairs with which my ongoing life is filled, the observation of thinking is a kind of exceptional state. This fact must be properly considered when it is a matter of determining the relationship of thinking to all other contents of observation. One must be clear about the fact that in the observation of thinking one is applying to it a way of doing things which constitutes the normal condition for the consideration of all other world content, but which, in the course of this normal state of affairs, does not take place with respect to thinking itself.

Someone could make the objection that what I have observed here about thinking also holds good for feeling and for our other spiritual activities. When we, for example, have the feeling of pleasure, this is kindled also by an object, and I observe in fact this object, but not the feeling of pleasure. This objection rests however upon an error. Pleasure stands by no means in the same relationship to its object as does the concept which thinking forms. I am conscious in the most definite way that the concept of a thing is formed through my activity, whereas pleasure is produced in me through an object in the same way as, for example, the change which a falling stone effects in an object upon which it falls. For observation, pleasure is a given in exactly the same way as the occurrence causing it. The same is not true of the concept. I can ask why a particular occurrence produces in me the feeling of pleasure. But I can by no means ask why an occurrence produces in me a particular sum of concepts. That would simply make no sense. In my reflecting on an occurrence it is not at all a question of an effect upon me. I can experience nothing about myself through the fact that I know the appropriate concepts for the observed change which a stone, thrown against a windowpane, causes in the latter. But I very much do experience something about my personality when I know the feeling which a particular occurrence awakens in me. When I say with respect to an observed object that this is a rose, I do not thereby say the slightest thing about myself; when, however, I say of the same thing that it gives me a feeling of pleasure, I

have characterized thereby not only the rose, but also
myself in my relationship to the rose.

To regard thinking and feeling as alike in their relationship to observation is therefore out of the question.
The same could also easily be demonstrated for the other
activities of the human spirit. They belong, in contrast to
thinking, in a category with other observed objects and
occurrences. It belongs precisely to the characteristic
nature of thinking that it is an activity which is directed
solely upon the observed object and not upon the thinking personality. This manifests itself already in the way
that we bring our thoughts about a thing to expression, in
contrast to our feelings or acts of will. When I see an object and know it to be a table, I will not usually say that I
am thinking about a table, but rather that this is a table.
But I will certainly say that I am pleased with the table.
In the first case it does not occur to me at all to express
the fact that I enter into relationship with the table; in the
second case, however, it is precisely a question of this
relationship. With the statement that I am thinking about
a table, I enter already into the exceptional state characterized above, in which something is made into an object
of observation that always accompanies and is contained
within our spiritual activity, but not as an observed object.

That is the characteristic nature of thinking, that the
thinker forgets his thinking while exercising it. It is not
thinking that occupies him, but rather the object of thinking that he is observing.

The first observation that we can make about thinking
is therefore this: that it is the unobserved element of our
ordinary spiritual life.

The reason why we do not observe thinking in our everyday spiritual life is none other than that it depends upon our own activity. What I do not myself bring forth comes as something objective into my field of observation. I see myself before it as before something that has occurred without me; it comes to me; I have to receive it as the prerequisite for my thinking process. While I am reflecting on the object, I am occupied with it; my gaze is turned to it. This occupation is in fact thinking contemplation. My attention is directed not upon my activity, but rather upon the object of this activity. In other words: while I am thinking, I do not look at my thinking, which I myself bring forth, but rather at the object of my thinking, which I do not bring forth.

I am, as a matter of fact, in the same position when I let the exceptional state arise and reflect on my thinking itself. I can never observe my present thinking; but rather I can only afterward make the experiences, which I have had about my thinking process, into the object of thinking. I would have to split myself into two personalities, into one who thinks, and into the other who looks on during this thinking itself, if I wanted to observe my present thinking. This I cannot do. I can only carry this out in two separate acts. The thinking that is to be observed is never the one active at the moment, but rather another one. Whether for this purpose I make my observations in connection with my own earlier thinking, or whether I follow the thought process of another person, or finally whether, as in the above case of the motion of billiard balls, I set up an imaginary thought process, does not matter.

Two things are incompatible with each other: active bringing forth and contemplative standing apart. This is recognized already in the first book of Moses. In the first six world–days God lets the world come forth, and only when it is there is the possibility present of looking upon it: "And God saw everything that He had made and, behold, it was very good." So it is also with our thinking. It must first be there if we want to observe it.

The reason it is impossible for us to observe thinking in its present course at a given moment is the same that allows us to know it more directly and more intimately than any other process of the world. Just because we bring it forth ourselves, we know the characteristics of its course, the way the happening to be considered takes place. What, in the other spheres of observation, can be found only in an indirect way—the factually corresponding connection, namely, and the interrelationship of the single objects—this we know in the case of thinking in a completely direct way. Why for my observation thunder follows lightning, I do not know at once; why my thinking joins the *concept* thunder with that of lightning, this I know directly out of the contents of the two concepts. Naturally the point is not at all whether I have the right concepts of lightning and thunder. The connection of those that I have is clear to me, and is so, in fact, through the concepts themselves.

This transparent clarity with respect to our thinking process is entirely independent of our knowledge about the physiological basis of thinking. I am speaking here about thinking insofar as it presents itself to the observa-

thinking, which we bring forth, as an object for our spiritual activity of thinking

tion of our spiritual activity.* How one material occurrence of my brain causes or influences another while I am carrying out a thought operation, does not come thereby at all into consideration. What I observe about thinking is not what occurrence in my brain joins the concept of lightning with that of thunder, but rather, what motivates me to bring the two concepts into a definite relationship. My observation shows that for my thought connections nothing is present for me by which to guide myself except the content of my thoughts; I do not guide myself by the material occurrences in my brain. For a less materialistic age than ours this observation would of course be altogether superfluous. In the present day, however, where there are people who believe that when we know what matter is we will also know how matter thinks, it must indeed be said that one may speak of thinking without heading right away into a collision with brain physiology. It is difficult for many people today to grasp the concept of thinking in its purity. Whoever raises as an objection to the picture of thinking painted here the statement of Cabanis that "The brain secretes thoughts as the liver does bile, the salivary glands saliva, etc.," simply does not know what I am talking about. He tries to find thinking through a mere process of observation in the same way as we proceed with other objects from the content of the world. He cannot find it in this way, however, because just there it eludes our normal observation as I have shown. A person who cannot overcome materialism

*geistigen Tätigkeit

lacks the ability to call forth the characterized exceptional state which brings to his consciousness what remains unconscious in all other spiritual activity.* With someone who does not have the good will to take this standpoint, one could as little speak about thinking as with a blind person about color. Still he should not believe that we regard physiological processes as thinking. He does not explain thinking, because he simply does not see it at all.

For everyone, however, who has the ability to observe thinking—and with good will every normally developed human being has it—this observation is the most important one he can possibly make. For he observes something that he himself brings forth; he does not see himself confronting an object at first foreign to him, but rather sees himself confronting his own activity. He knows how what he is observing comes about. He sees into its relationships and interconnections. A firm point has been won from which one can seek, with well-founded hope, the explanation of the rest of world phenomena.

The feeling of having such a firm point caused the founder of modern philosophy, Descartes, to base all human knowing upon the statement, *I think, therefore I am.* All other things, everything else that happens is there without me; I do not know whether as truth, whether as illusion and dream. There is only one thing I know with altogether unqualified certainty, for I myself bring it to its certain existence: my thinking. Though it may have still another source of its existence, though it may come from God or from somewhere else; that it is there in that

*Geistestätigkeit

sense in which I myself bring it forth, of this I am certain. Descartes had at first no justification for imputing another meaning to his statement. He could only maintain that, within the content of the world I grasp myself in my thinking as within an activity most inherently my own. What the attached *therefore I am* is supposed to mean has been much disputed. It can mean something, however, on one condition only. The simplest statement I can make about a thing is that it *is*, that it exists. How then this existence is to be more closely determined cannot be stated right away with respect to anything that comes onto the horizon of my experiences. One must first examine every object in its relationship to others, in order to be able to determine in which sense it can be spoken of as something existing. An occurrence one experiences may be a sum of perceptions, but also a dream, a hallucination, and so on. In short, I cannot say in which sense it exists. This I cannot conclude from the occurrence itself, but rather I will learn this when I look at the occurrence in relation to other things. There again, however, I can know no *more* than how it stands in relation to these things. My searching first comes onto firm ground when I find an object from which I can derive the sense of its existence out of it itself. This I am myself, however, in that I think, for I give to my existence the definite, self-sustaining content of thinking activity. Now I can take my start from there and ask whether the other things exist in the same or in a different sense.

When one makes thinking the object of observation, one adds to the rest of the observed content of the world something that otherwise eludes one's attention; one does not change, however, the way in which the human being conducts himself, also with respect to the other things. One adds to the number of objects of observation, but not to the method of observation. While we are observing the other things, there is mingling with world happening* (to which I now reckon observation as well)—a process that is overlooked. There is something present, different from all other happening, that is not taken into account. When I look at my thinking, however, there is no such element present that has not been taken into account. For, what is hovering now in the background is itself again only thinking. The observed object is qualitatively the same as the activity that directs itself upon it. And that is again a unique characteristic of thinking. When we make it an object to be looked at, we do not find ourselves compelled to do this with the help of something qualitatively different, but rather we can remain within the same element.

When I weave into my thinking an object given without my participation, I go beyond my observation, and the question becomes: What gives me the right to do this? Why do I not simply let the object affect me? In what way is it possible that my thinking has a relation to the object? Those are the questions which each person must ask himself who reflects upon his own thought processes. They fall away when one reflects upon thinking itself. We add to thinking nothing foreign to it, and therefore do not also have to justify any such addition to ourselves.

*Weltgeschehen

Schelling says that to know nature means to create nature.—Whoever takes literally these words of this bold Naturphilosoph will certainly have to renounce all knowledge of nature forever. For nature is already there once, and in order to create it a second time one must know the principles by which it has arisen. For a nature that one wanted first to create, one would have to detect, from the nature already existing, the conditions of its existence. This detecting, that would have to precede the creating, would however be knowing nature, and would indeed still be knowing nature in the case where, after the detecting is completed, the creating did not take place at all. Only a nature not yet present could one create *before* knowing it.

What is impossible with respect to nature, namely, creating before knowing, we do accomplish with respect to thinking. If we wanted to wait with thinking until we knew it, we would never come to it. We must resolutely proceed with thinking, in order afterward, by means of observation of what we ourselves have done, to come to knowledge of it. We ourselves first create an object for thinking to observe. The existence of all other objects has been provided without our participation.

Someone could easily oppose my statement that we must think before we can look at thinking, with another, and consider it equally valid, namely, that we cannot wait with digesting either until we have observed the occurrence of digestion. That would be similar to the objection which Pascal made to Descartes when he declared that one could also say, "I take a walk, therefore I am." Certainly I must also resolutely digest before I have studied the physiological process of digestion. But that could only be compared with looking at thinking if I did not afterward want to look, in thinking, at the digestion, but rather wanted to eat and digest it. And it is in fact not without reason that while digestion cannot become the object of digestion, thinking can very well become the object of thinking.

It is therefore beyond any doubt that in thinking we grasp world happening by one tip where we must be present if something is to come about. And that is after all exactly the point. That is exactly the reason why things confront me as such a riddle: because I am so uninvolved in their coming about. I simply find them before me; with thinking, however, I know how it is done. Thus there is no starting point for looking at all world happening more primal than thinking.

I would like still to mention a widespread error prevailing with respect to thinking. It consists in the statement that thinking, as it is in itself, is nowhere given us. The thinking which joins the observations we make of our experiences and interweaves them with a web of concepts, is said to be not at all the same as that thinking which we afterwards lift out of the objects of observation again and make the object of our study. What we first weave unconsciously into the things is said to be something entirely different from what we then extricate from them again with consciousness.

Whoever draws these conclusions does not grasp the fact that it is not possible at all for him to escape thinking in this way. I absolutely cannot get outside of thinking if I want to look at thinking. If one makes a distinction between thinking as it is prior to my consciousness of it, and the thinking of which I am afterwards conscious, one should not then forget, in doing so, that this distinction is entirely superficial and has absolutely nothing to do with the matter itself. I do not in any way make a thing into a different one through the fact that I look at it in thinking. I can imagine that a being with sense organs of a completely different sort and with an intelligence that functions differently would have an entirely different mental picture of a horse than I do, but I cannot imagine to myself that my own thinking becomes a different one through the fact that I observe it. I myself observe what I myself carry out. How my thinking looks to an intelligence other than my own is not the question now; the question here is how it looks to me. In any case, however, the picture of *my* thinking within another intelligence cannot be truer than my own picture. Only if I were not myself the thinking being, but rather were to approach the thinking as an activity of a being foreign to me, could I say that my picture of the thinking arises in a particular way, but that I could not know how the thinking of the being in itself is.

But so far there is not the slightest motivation for me to look upon my own thinking from another standpoint. I consider, indeed, all the rest of the world with the help of thinking. How should I make an exception to this in the case of my thinking?

With this I consider it to be well enough justified that I take my start from thinking in my consideration of the world. When Archimedes had discovered the lever, he believed that, with its help, he could lift the whole cosmos

from its hinges, if he could only find a point upon which
to rest his instrument. He needed something that is supported through itself, not through something else. In
thinking we have a principle that exists in and through
itself. Let us start here in our attempt to comprehend the
world. Thinking we can grasp through thinking itself.
The question is only whether through it we can also ap-
prehend something else as well.

I have spoken until now about thinking without taking any account of its bearer, human consciousness. Most
philosophers of the present day will object that, before
there can be a thinking, there must be a consciousness.
Therefore consciousness and not thinking should be the
starting point. There would be no thinking without consciousness. I must reply to this that if I want to clarify
what the relationship is between thinking and consciousness, I must think about it. I thereby presuppose thinking. Now one can certainly respond to this that if the
philosopher wants to *understand* consciousness, he then
makes use of thinking; to this extent he does presuppose
it; in the usual course of life, however, thinking arises
within consciousness and thereby presupposes it. If this
answer were given to the world creator, who wanted to
create thinking, it would without a doubt be justified.
One cannot of course let thinking arise without having
brought about consciousness beforehand. For the philosopher, however, it is not a matter of creating the world,
but of understanding it. He must therefore seek the starting point not for creating, but rather for understanding
the world. I find it altogether strange when someone re-
proaches the philosopher for concerning himself before

all else with the correctness of his principles, rather than working immediately with the objects he wants to understand. The world creator had to know above all how he could find a bearer for thinking; the philosopher, however, must seek a sure basis from which he can understand what is already there. What good does it do us to start with consciousness and to subject it to our thinking contemplation, if we know nothing beforehand about the possibility of gaining insight into things through *thinking* contemplation?

We must first of all look at thinking in a completely neutral way, without any relationship to a thinking subject or conceived object. For in subject and object we already have concepts that are formed through thinking. It is undeniable that, *before other things can be understood, thinking must be understood.* Whoever does deny this, overlooks the fact that he, as human being, is not a first member of creation but its last member. One cannot, therefore, in order to explain the world through concepts, start with what are in time the first elements of existence, but rather with what is most immediately and intimately given us. We cannot transfer ourselves with one bound to the beginning of the world in order to begin our investigations there; we must rather start from the present moment and see if we can ascend from the later to the earlier. As long as geology spoke of imagined revolutions in order to explain the present state of the earth, it was groping in the dark. Only when it took as its starting point the investigation of processes which are presently still at work on the earth and drew conclusions about the past from these, did it gain firm ground. As long as philosophy assumes all kinds of principles, such as atom, motion, matter, will, or the unconscious, it will hover in the air. Only when the philosopher regards the absolute last as his first, can he reach his goal. This absolute last, however, to which world evolution has come, is *thinking.*

There are people who say that we cannot, however, really determine with certainty whether our thinking is in itself correct or not. That to this extent, therefore, the starting point remains in any case a dubious one. That makes exactly as much sense as it would to harbor a doubt as to whether a tree is in itself correct or not. Thinking is a fact; and to speak of the correctness or incorrectness of a fact makes no sense. At most I can have doubts about whether thinking is put to a correct use, just as I can doubt whether a particular tree will provide wood appropriate for use in a certain tool. To show to what extent my use of thinking with respect to the world is a correct or incorrect one is precisely the task of this book. I can understand it if someone harbors doubt that something can be determined about the world through thinking; but it is incomprehensible to me how someone can doubt the correctness of thinking in itself.

Addendum to the Revised Edition of 1918. In the preceding considerations the momentous difference between thinking and all other soul activities is pointed to as a fact that reveals itself to a really unprejudiced observation. Whoever does not strive for this unprejudiced observation will be tempted to raise objections against these considerations like the following: When I think about a rose, this still expresses only a relationship of my "I" to the rose, just as when I feel the beauty of the rose. There exists in exactly the same way a relationship between "I" and object in thinking as there is for example in feeling or perceiving. Whoever makes this objection does not take into consideration that *only* in the activity of thinking does the "I" know itself to be of *one* being with what is active, right into every ramification of the activity. With no other soul activity is this absolutely the case. When, for example, a pleasure is felt, a more sensitive observation can very well distinguish to what extent the "I" knows itself as one with something active, and to what extent something passive is present in the "I" in such a way that the pleasure merely happens to the "I." And it is also like this with the other soul activities. One should only not confuse "having thought pictures" with working through thoughts in thinking. Thought pictures can arise in the soul in a dream-like way, like vague intimations. This is not *thinking.*—To be sure, someone could say now that if thinking is meant in this way, then will is present in thinking, and one has then to do not merely with thinking, but also with the will in thinking. This, however, would only justify us in saying that real thinking must always be willed. But this has nothing to do with the characterization of thinking made in this book. The nature of thinking may in fact necessitate that thinking be *willed*; the point is that nothing is willed which, as it is taking place, does not appear before the "I" as totally its own surveyable activity. One must even say in fact, *because of* the nature of thinking presented here, that thinking appears to the observer as *willed*, through and through. Whoever makes an effort really to see into everything that comes into consideration for an evaluation of thinking, cannot but perceive that the characteristic spoken of here does apply to this soul activity.

A personality valued very highly as a thinker by the author of this book has raised the objection that thinking cannot be spoken of in the way it is done here, because what one believes oneself to be observing as active thinking is only a semblance. In actuality one is observing only the result of an unconscious activity that underlies thinking. Only because this unconscious activity is in fact not observed, does the illusion arise that the observed thinking exists in and through itself, in the same way that one believes one sees a motion when a line of single electric sparks is set off in quick succession. This objection is also based upon an inexact view of the actual situation. Whoever makes it does not take into account that it is the ''I'' itself that, standing *within* thinking, observes *its* own activity. The ''I'' would have to stand outside of thinking if it could be fooled as in the case of the quick succession of the light of electric sparks. One could go still further and say that whoever makes such an analogy is deluding himself mightily, like someone, for example, who truly wanted to maintain of a light in motion, that it is newly lit, by unknown hand, at every point where it appears.— No, whoever wants to see in thinking something other than that which is brought forth within the ''I'' itself as a surveyable activity, such a person would have to first blind himself to the plain facts observable before him, in order then to be able to base thinking upon a hypothetical activity. Whoever does not blind himself in this way must recognize that everything which he ''thinks onto'' thinking in this way leads him out of the being of thinking. Unprejudiced observation shows that nothing can be attributed to the being of thinking that is not found *within* thinking itself. One cannot come to something that *causes* thinking, if one leaves the realm of thinking.

IV
The World as Perception

Through thinking, *concepts* and *ideas* arise. What a
concept is cannot be said in words. Words can only make
the human being aware of the fact that he has concepts.
When someone sees a tree, his thinking reacts to his
observation; to the object there comes then an ideal counterpart, and he regards the object and ideal counterpart
as belonging together. When the object disappears from
his field of observation, there remains behind only its
ideal counterpart. The latter is the concept of the object.
The more our experience broadens, the greater the sum
of our concepts becomes. The concepts however by no
means stand there isolated. They join themselves together
into a lawful whole. The concept "organism" joins itself,
for example, to the others of "lawful development" and
"growth." Other concepts formed in connection with
single things merge totally into one. All the concepts that
I make for myself of lions merge together into the overall
concept "lion." In this way the individual concepts join
themselves into a united system of concepts within which
every one has its particular place. Ideas are not qualitative-

ly different from concepts. They are only concepts that are fuller in content, more saturated, and wider in scope. I must particularly emphasize that heed be taken at this point of the fact that I have indicated *thinking* as my starting point and not *concepts* and *ideas*, which are first gained through thinking. These already presuppose thinking. What I have said therefore about the self-sustaining and self-determined nature of thinking cannot simply be transferred to concepts. (I state this here expressly, because herein lies my difference with Hegel. He posits the concept as primary and original.)

The concept cannot be gained from observation. This is already evident from the fact that the maturing human being only slowly and gradually forms his concepts for the objects which surround him. The concepts are added to the observation.

A widely read philosopher of the present day, Herbert Spencer, describes the mental process we carry out with respect to an observation in the following way:

"If, when walking through the fields some day in September you hear a rustle a few yards in advance, and, on observing the ditch-side where it occurs, see the herbage agitated, you will probably turn toward the spot to learn by what this sound and motion are produced. As you approach there flutters into the ditch a partridge; on seeing which your curiosity is satisfied—you have .what you call an *explanation* of the appearances. The explanation, mark, amounts to this; that whereas throughout life you have had countless experiences of disturbance among small stationary bodies, accompanying the movement of other bodies among them, and have generalized the rela-

tion between such disturbances and such movements, you consider this particular disturbance explained on finding it to present an instance of the like relation."*
When viewed more closely the matter turns out to be completely different from what is described here. When I hear a sound, I seek first of all the concept corresponding to this observation. It is only this concept that first takes me beyond the sound. Whoever does not reflect further just hears the sound and is content with that. Through my reflection, however, it is clear to me that I have to comprehend a sound as an effect. Therefore, only when I join the concept *effect* with the perception of the sound, am I moved to go beyond the individual observation and seek the *cause.* The concept "effect" calls up the concept "cause," and I then look for the causal object, which I find in the form of the partridge. These concepts, "cause" and "effect," however, I can never gain through mere observation, no matter how many instances it may cover. Observation calls forth thinking, and this latter first shows me the way to join the single experience to another.

If one demands of a "strictly objective science" that it take its content only from observation, one must demand at the same time that it renounce all thinking. Because thinking by its very nature goes beyond what is observed.

This is the place now to pass from thinking to the being who thinks. For, through him thinking is joined with observation. Human consciousness is the stage upon which concept and observation meet each other and where they become joined. But this (human) consciousness is

First Principles, Part I, Par. 23.

thereby characterized at the same time. It is the mediator between thinking and observation. Insofar as the human being observes a thing, this thing appears to him as given; insofar as he thinks, he appears to himself as active. He considers the thing as *object*, himself as the thinking *subject*. Because he focuses his thinking upon the observation, he has consciousness of the objects; because he directs his thinking upon himself, he has consciousness of himself or *self-consciousness*. Human consciousness must necessarily be self-consciousness at the same time, because it is *thinking* consciousness. For when thinking directs its gaze upon its own activity, it then has its own inmost being, its subject, as object before it.

But the fact must not be overlooked now that it is only with the help of thinking that we are able to designate ourselves as subject and to set ourselves over against objects. Therefore thinking must never be considered to be a merely subjective activity. Thinking is *beyond* subject and object. It forms these two concepts just as much as all others. When we as thinking subject, therefore, relate the concept to an object, we must not, in so doing, consider this relationship to be something merely subjective. It is not the subject that brings about the relationship, but rather thinking. The subject does not think by virtue of being subject, but rather appears to itself as a subject because it is able to think. The activity which the human being, as *thinking* entity, exercises is therefore no merely subjective one, but rather one that is neither subjective nor objective, one that goes beyond these two concepts. I must never say that my individual subject thinks; it is much more the case that my subject itself lives by the grace of thinking. Thinking is an element that leads me out of and above my self, and joins me with objects. But it separates me from them at the same time, inasmuch as it places me over against them as subject.

This is the basis for the double nature of the human being: he thinks and thereby encompasses himself and the rest of the world; but he must, by means of thinking, at the same time designate himself as an individual that stands over and against the things.

The next thing will now be to ask ourselves how the other element—which we have up to now merely called object of observation, and which encounters thinking within our consciousness—come into our consciousness?

In order to answer this question we must exclude from our field of observation everything that has already been brought into it through thinking. For our content of consciousness at any given moment is already permeated with concepts in the most manifold way.

We must picture to ourselves a being with fully developed human intelligence arising out of nothingness and approaching the world. What he would become aware of in it, before he brought his thinking into activity, is the pure content of observation. The world would then show this being only the bare aggregate, without interconnection, of the *objects of sensation*: colors, tones, sensations of pressure, warmth, taste, and smell; then feelings of pleasure and displeasure. This aggregate is the content of pure observation without thoughts. Over against it stands thinking, which is ready to unfold its activity when a point of attack is found. Experience soon teaches us that a point is found. Thinking is capable of drawing threads from one element of observation to the other. Thinking connects definite concepts with these elements and brings them thereby into a relationship. We have already seen above, how a sound confronting us is joined with another observation through the fact that we designate the former as the effect of the latter.

When we now recall that the activity of thinking is absolutely not to be taken as subjective, we will thus also not be tempted to believe that such connections, established through thinking, have a merely subjective validity.

It will now be a matter, through thinking consideration, of seeking the connection which the directly given content of observation described above has to our conscious subject.

Because of the variability in the use of language it seems advisable for me to come to an understanding with my reader about the use of a word which I will have to employ in what follows. I will call the immediate objects of sensation enumerated above *perceptions*, insofar as the conscious subject takes cognizance of them through observation. I therefore use this word to indicate, not the process of observation, but rather the *object* of this observation.

I do not choose the term *sensation*, because in physiology this has a definite meaning that is narrower than my concept of perception. An emotion within myself can certainly be called a perception, but not a sensation in the physiological sense. I come to know even my emotions through their becoming *perceptions* for me. And the way we come to know our thinking through observation is such, that we can also use the word perception for thinking as it first appears to our consciousness.

The naive person considers his perceptions, in the

way they immediately appear to him, as things having an
existence completely independent of him. When he sees a
tree, he believes right away that it is standing there in
that spot toward which his gaze is directed, in the shape
he sees, with the colors its parts have, etc. When the same
person sees the sun appear in the morning as a disk on the
horizon, and follows the course of this disk, he believes
that all this exists and occurs in this way (in and for itself),
just as he observes it to. He holds fast to his belief, until
he meets other perceptions that contradict his former
ones. The child, who does not yet have any experience of
distance, reaches for the moon, and corrects the way he
had first seen it to be only when a second perception is
found to be in contradiction with the first. Every broadening of the circle of my perception obliges me to correct
my picture of the world. This is evident in daily life just
as much as in the spiritual development of mankind. The
picture which the ancients made for themselves of the
relationship of the earth to the sun and to the other
heavenly bodies, had to be replaced by Copernicus with
another one, because it did not accord with perceptions
unknown to earlier times. A man born blind said, after
Dr. Franz had operated on him, that before his operation
he had formed a completely different picture of the size
of objects through the perceptions of his sense of touch.
He had to correct his perceptions of touch through his
perceptions of sight.

How is it that we are compelled to make such continuous corrections of our observations?

A simple reflection brings the answer to this question.
When I am standing at one end of an avenue of trees, the

trees distant from me at the other end appear to me
smaller and closer together than they do where I am standing. My perceptual picture becomes a different one when
I change the place from which I make my observations.
This picture, therefore, in the form in which it approaches
me, is dependent upon a determining factor which is not
due to the object, but which rather is attributable to me,
the one doing the perceiving. For an avenue of trees it is a
matter of complete indifference where I am standing.
The picture, however, that I receive of it, is essentially
dependent upon where I am standing. In the same way it
is a matter of indifference to the sun and to the planetary
system that human beings happen to view them from the
earth. The perceptual picture, however, which presents
itself to human beings is determined through this their
dwelling place. This dependency of our perceptual picture upon our point of observation is the one that is
easiest to recognize. The matter becomes more difficult,
to be sure, when we learn to know the dependency of our
perceptual world upon our bodily and spiritual organization. The physicist shows us that within the space in
which we hear a sound, vibrations of the air take place,
and that the body also, in which we seek the origin of the
sound, exhibits a vibrating movement of its parts. We only
perceive this movement as sound if we have a normally
organized ear. Without such an ear the whole world would
remain forever silent for us. Physiology teaches us that
there are people who perceive nothing of the magnificent
splendor of color that surrounds us. Their perceptual picture evinces only nuances of light and dark. Others do
not perceive only one particular color, such as red, for ex-

ample. This shade is missing from their world picture, which is therefore actually a different one than that of the average person. I would like to call the dependency of my perceptual picture upon my place of observation, "mathematical," and the dependency upon my organization "qualitative." Through the former, the size relationships and respective distances of my perceptions are determined; through the latter, the quality of my perceptions. That I see a red surface as red—this qualitative determination—depends upon the organization of my eye.

My perceptual pictures are therefore at first subjective. Knowledge of the subjective character of our perceptions can easily lead to doubt as to whether anything objective underlies them at all. When we know that a perception—of a red color, for example, or of a particular tone—is not possible without a definite structure in our organism, one can arrive at the belief that this perception, apart from our subjective organism, has no reality, that the perception has no kind of existence without the act of perceiving, whose object it is. This view has found a classic proponent in George Berkeley, who was of the opinion that the human being, from the moment he has become conscious of the significance of the subject for the perception, can no longer believe in a world that is present without the conscious mind. He says, "Some truths there are, so near and obvious to the mind that man need only open his eyes to see them. Such I take this important one to be, to wit, that all the choir of heaven and furniture of the earth, in a word, all those bodies which compose the mighty frame of the world, have not any subsistence without a mind, that their *being is* to be perceived or known; that, consequently, so long as they are not actually perceived by me, or do not exist in my mind or that of any other *created spirit*, they must either have no existence at all, *or else subsist in the mind of some eternal spirit.''** For this view, nothing more of the perception remains, if one disregards the fact of its being perceived. There is no color when none is seen, no tone when none is heard. Just as little as color and tone, do dimension, shape, and motion exist outside of the <u>act of</u> perception. We nowhere see bare dimension or shape, but always see them connected with color or with other characteristics which indisputably depend upon our subjectivity. If these latter characteristics disappear along with our perception, then that must also be the case for the elements of dimension or shape that are bound to them.

An objection can be made that, even if figure, color, tone, etc. do have no existence other than within my act of perception, there must still be things which are there without my consciousness and to which my conscious perceptual pictures are similar; to this objection the above view responds by saying that a color can only be similar to a color, a figure similar to a figure. Our perceptions can only be similar to our perceptions, but not to any other things. Even what we call an object is nothing other than a group of perceptions which are connected in a definite way. If I take away from a table its shape, dimensions, color, etc.—everything, in short, that is only my perception—then nothing more remains. This view,

Principles of Human Knowledge, Part I, Section 6.

consistently pursued, leads to the opinion that the objects
of my perceptions are present only through me, and indeed only insofar as, and as long as, I perceive them; they
disappear along with my act of perceiving and have no
meaning without it. Other than my perceptions I know of
no objects, however, and can know of none.

No objection can be brought against this opinion as
long as I am merely bringing into consideration in a
general way the fact that the perception is codetermined
by the organization of my subject. The matter would present itself in an essentially different way, however, if we
were able to say what the function of our perceiving is in
the genesis of a perception. We would then know what is
happening with the perception during the act of perceiving, and could also determine what about it would
already have to exist, before it is perceived.

With this, our consideration of the object of perception leads over to the subject of perception. I do not perceive other things only; I also perceive my self. The perception of my self has at first the content that I am what
endures in the face of perceptual pictures that continually
come and go. The perception of my "I" can always appear
in my consciousness while I am having other perceptions.
When I am absorbed in the perception of a given object, I
have for the moment only a consciousness of it. To this
can then come the perception of my self. I am from then
on conscious not merely of the object, but also of my personality, which stands before the object and observes it. I
do not merely see a tree, but I also know that *it is I* who
see it. I recognize also that something is occurring within
me while I observe the tree. When the tree disappears

from my field of vision, something of this occurrence remains behind for my consciousness: a picture of the tree.
During my observation this picture has connected itself
with my self. My self has become richer; its content has
acquired a new element. This element I call my *mental
picture** of the tree. I would never be in a position to
speak of *mental pictures*, if I did not experience them
within the perception of my self. Perceptions would come
and go; I would let them pass before me. Only because I
perceive my self and notice that *its* content also changes
with every perception, do I see myself compelled to bring
my observation of the object into relationship with my own
change in condition, and to speak of my mental picture.

I perceive the mental picture connected to my self in
the same sense as I perceive color, tone, etc. connected to
other objects. I can also now make the distinction of calling these other objects which come before me *outer world*,
while I designate the content of my self-perception as *inner
world*. Misconceptions about the relationship of mental
picture and object have brought about the greatest misunderstandings in modern philosophy. The perception of
a change in us, the modification that my self undergoes,
was pushed into the foreground, and the object causing
this modification was totally lost from view. One said that
we do not perceive the objects, but only our mental pictures. I supposedly know nothing about the table-in-itself,
which is the object of my observation, but only about the
change which takes place with my self while I am perceiving the table. This view should not be confused with that

---

*Vorstellung (often translated ''representation'')

of Berkeley mentioned before. Berkeley maintains the subjective nature of the content of my perception, but he does not say I can only know about my mental pictures. He limits my knowledge to my mental pictures, because he is of the opinion that there are no objects outside of mental picturing. What I look upon as a table is for Berkeley no longer present as soon as I no longer direct my gaze upon it. Therefore Berkeley lets my perceptions arise directly through the power of God. I see a table because God calls forth this perception within me. Berkeley thus knows no other real beings except God and human spirits. What we call world is present only within spirits. What the naive person calls outer world, physical nature, does not exist for Berkeley. Over against this view there stands the Kantian one now predominating, which limits our knowledge of the world to our mental pictures, not because it is convinced that there can be nothing apart from our mental pictures, but because it believes us to be so organized that we can experience only the changes of our own self and not the things-in-themselves which cause these changes. From the fact that I know only my mental pictures, this view concludes not that there is no existence independent of these mental pictures, but only that the subject cannot take up such an existence directly into itself; it can do nothing with it except through the "medium of his subjective thoughts, to imagine it, to suppose it, to think it, to know it, or perhaps also not to know it" (O. Liebmann, *Contribution to the Analysis of Reality**). This view believes it is saying some-

---

**Zur Analysis der Wirklichkeit*

thing absolutely certain, something directly obvious without any proof. "The first fundamental principle which the philosopher has to bring to distinct consciousness for himself consists in the recognition that our knowledge *at first* extends itself to nothing beyond our mental pictures. Our mental pictures are the only thing that we know directly, experience directly; and, just because we experience them directly, it is the case that even the most radical doubt cannot tear away from us our knowledge of our mental pictures. On the other hand, knowledge that goes beyond our mental picturing—whenever I use this expression I mean it in the widest sense, so that all psychic happenings come under it—is not secure from doubt. Therefore, *at the beginning of any philosophizing*, all knowledge which goes beyond our mental pictures must be expressly presented as doubtful"; thus Volkelt begins his book on *Immanuel Kant's Epistemology.* What is here presented in this way, as though it were an immediate and obvious truth, is in reality, however, the result of a thought-operation that runs as follows: The naive person believes that the objects, in the way he perceives them, are also present outside of his consciousness. Physics, physiology, and psychology seem to teach, however, that for our perceptions our organization is necessary, that we consequently can know about nothing except what our organization transmits to us from the things. Our perceptions are thus modifications of our organization, not things-in-themselves. Eduard von Hartmann has characterized the train of thought indicated here as in fact the one which must convince us of the principle that we can have a direct knowledge only of our mental pictures (see his *Basic Problem of Epistemology**). Because, outside of our organism, we find vibrations of physical bodies and of the air which manifest to us as sound, it is concluded that what we call sound is nothing more than a subjective reaction of our organism to those motions in the outer world. In the same way one finds that color and warmth are only modifications of our organism. And one is in fact of the view that these two kinds of perceptions are called forth in us through the effect of occurrences in the outer world which are utterly different from what our warmth or color experience is. When such occurrences stimulate the nerves in my skin, I have the subjective perception of warmth; when such occurrences encounter the optic nerve, I perceive light and color. Light, color, and warmth, therefore, are that with which my sensory nerves respond to the stimuli from outside. Even my sense of touch transmits to me, not the objects of the outer world, but only my own states. In the sense of modern physics one could think, for example, that bodies consist of infinitely small particles, of molecules, and that these molecules do not border directly upon each other, but rather are at certain distances from each other. Between them, therefore, is empty space. Across these distances the molecules act upon each other by means of forces of attraction and repulsion. When I bring my hand toward a body, the molecules of my hand by no means directly touch those of the body, but rather there remains a certain distance between body and hand; and what I sense as the body's resistance is nothing more than the effect of the force of

---

**Das Grundproblem der Erkenntnistheorie*

repulsion which its molecules exert upon my hand. I am altogether outside the body and only perceive its effect upon my organism.

The doctrine put forward by J. Müller (1801–1858) about the so-called specific sense energies complements these reflections. It consists in declaring that each sense organ has the characteristic of responding to all outer stimuli in one specific way only. If the optic nerve is acted upon, a perception of light arises, no matter whether the stimulus occurs through what we call light, or whether a mechanical pressure or an electric current affects the nerve. Furthermore, different perceptions are called forth in the different sense organs by the same outer stimuli. This seems to indicate that our senses can transmit only what occurs within them, but nothing of the outer world. The senses, each according to its nature, determine the perceptions.

Physiology shows that a direct knowledge of what the objects cause to happen within our sense organs is also out of the question. As the physiologist pursues the occurrences in our own body, he finds that, already in the sense organs, the effects of an outer motion are transformed in the most manifold way. We see that most distinctly with the eye and ear. Both are very complicated organs which essentially change the outer stimulus before they bring it to the corresponding nerve. From the peripheral end of the nerve, the already changed stimulus is now conducted further to the brain. Here first of all the central organs must be stimulated again. From this is inferred that the outer occurrence has undergone a series of transformations before it comes to consciousness. What takes place in the brain is connected with the outer occurrence through so many intermediary occurrences that any similarity between the two is inconceivable. What the brain finally communicates to the soul are neither outer occurrences nor occurrences in the sense organs, but only such as are in the brain. But the soul still does not perceive even these directly. What we finally have in our consciousness are not brain processes at all, but rather *sensations*. My sensation of *red* has absolutely no similarity to the process which takes place in my brain when I experience the red. The latter only appears again in the soul as an effect and is only caused by the brain process. Therefore Hartmann says (*The Basic Problem of Epistemology*), "What the subject perceives are therefore always only modifications of his own psychic states and nothing else." When I have sensations these are, however, still far from being grouped together into what I perceive as the things. Only single sensations, after all, can be communicated to me through the brain. The sensations of hard and soft are communicated to me through the sense of touch, sensations of color and light through the sense of sight. In spite of this the sensations find themselves united upon one and the same object. This union must therefore first be accomplished by the soul itself. This means that the soul assembles into physical objects the single sensations communicated through the brain. My brain transmits to me individually my sensations of sight, touch, and hearing—and does this, indeed, along entirely different paths—which my soul then assembles into the mental picture "trumpet." It is this last part (mental picture of the trumpet) of a process that, for my conscious-

ness, is given first of all. There is in this last part nothing
more to be found of what is outside me and originally
made an impression on my senses. The external object,
on its way to the brain, and through the brain to the soul,
has been entirely lost.

It would be difficult to find another edifice of thought
in the history of the spiritual life of man which has been
assembled with keener thought, and which nevertheless
crumbles into nothingness upon closer examination. Let
us take a closer look at the way it is built up. One starts
first of all with what is given to naive consciousness, with
the thing that is perceived. Then one shows that everything belonging to this thing would not be there for us if
we had no senses. No eye: no color. Therefore the color is
not yet present in that which works upon the eye. The
color first arises through the interaction of the eye with
the object. The latter is therefore colorless. But the color
is also not present in the eye; for in it a chemical or
physical process is present, which is first led to the brain
through a nerve, and which there causes another process.
Even this is not yet the color. The color is first called
forth, through the brain process, within the soul. There
the color still does not enter into my consciousness, but
rather is first transferred outward by the soul onto a body.
On this body I believe I finally perceive the color. We
have made a complete circle. We become conscious of a
colored body. That is first. Now the thought operation
commences. If I had no eye, the body would be colorless
for me. Thus, I cannot attribute the color to the body. I
take up the search for the color. I look for it in the eye: in
vain; in the nerve: in vain; in the brain: also in vain; in

the soul: here I do find it, in fact, but not connected with the body. I find the colored body again only where I took my start. The circle is closed. I believe that I now recognize as a creation of my soul, what the naive person believes to be present outside in space.

As long as one stops here, everything seems to be in excellent shape. But the matter must be taken up once more from the beginning. Until now I have been dealing with an object: with the outer perception about which earlier, as a naive person, I had a completely incorrect view. I was of the opinion that the perception had an objective existence, in the form that I perceive it. Now I notice that the perception disappears along with my mental picturing, that it is only a modification of my soul state. Now do I still have any right at all to start with the perception in my considerations? Can I say of the perception that it acts upon my soul? From now on I must treat the table, which I earlier believed acted upon me and brought forth a mental picture of itself in me, itself as a mental picture. But then my sense organs and the processes in them are also merely subjective. I have no right to speak of a real eye, but only of my mental picture of an eye. It is just the same with the nerves and the brain process, and no less so with the occurrence in the soul itself through which things are supposedly built up out of the chaos of manifold sensations. If, under the assumption of the correctness of the first circle of thought, I run through once more the parts of my act of knowledge, the latter shows itself to be a web of mental pictures that, as such, certainly cannot act upon each other. I cannot say that my mental picture of the object acts upon my mental picture of the eye and that out of this interaction emerges my mental picture of the color. But I also do not need to do this. For as soon as it is clear to me that my sense organs and their activity, my nerve and soul process, can also only be given me through perception, the train of thought described above reveals itself in its full impossibility. It is correct that for me there is no perception without the corresponding sense organ. But just as little is there a sense organ without perception. I can go over from my perception of the table to the eye that sees it, to the nerves of the hand which touch it; but what occurs within these I can again learn only from perception. And there I soon notice then that in the process which takes place in the eye, there is not a trace of similarity with what I perceive as color. I cannot do away with my perception of color just by showing the process in the eye that takes place in it during this perception. Just as little do I find the color again within the processes of the nerves and brain; I only connect new perceptions within my organism to the first ones which the naive person places outside his organism. I only go from one perception to another.

Moreover, there is a break in this whole line of reasoning. I am in a position to follow the occurrences in my organism up to the processes in my brain, even though my conclusions become ever more hypothetical the more I approach the central occurrences of the brain. The path of *external* observation ends with the occurrences in my brain, with that occurrence, in fact, which I would perceive if I could study the brain with the help of physical and chemical means and methods. The path of *inner* observation begins with the sensation and extends to the construction of things out of the material of sensation. In the transition from brain process to sensation the path of observation is broken.

The way of thinking characterized here, which calls itself "critical idealism" in contradistinction to the standpoint of the naive consciousness which it calls "naive realism," makes the mistake of characterizing the *one* perception as mental picture, while accepting the other in the very same sense as does the naive realism which it seemingly had refuted. This way of thinking wants to prove that perceptions have the character of mental pictures, by accepting in naive fashion the perceptions made of one's own organism as objectively valid facts, and in all this still overlooking the fact that it is throwing together two realms of observation, between which it can find no mediation.

Critical idealism can refute naive realism only if it itself accepts, in naive realistic fashion, that one's own organism exists objectively. The moment it becomes conscious of the total similarity in nature between the perceptions made of one's own organism and the perceptions accepted by naive realism as existing objectively, it can no longer base itself upon the first kind of perceptions as though they afforded a sure foundation. It would also have to regard one's subjective organization as a mere complex of mental pictures. In so doing, however, it would lose the possibility of thinking that the content of the perceived world is caused by one's spiritual organization. One would have to assume that the mental picture "color" is only a modification of the mental picture "eye." So-called critical idealism cannot be proven without borrowing from naive realism. The latter is only refuted through the fact that one accepts naive realism's own presuppositions as valid in another area, without examining them there.

From all this, it is certain, at least, that critical idealism cannot be proven through investigations within the realm of perception, and that thereby perception cannot be divested of its objective character.

But even less can the thesis, *"The perceived world is my mental picture,"* be presented as obvious in itself and needing no proof. Schopenhauer begins his principal work, *The World as Will and Mental Picture,** with the words: "The world is my mental picture:—this is the truth which is valid with respect to every living and knowing being, even though man alone can bring it into reflective abstract consciousness; and if he really does this, then philosophical enlightenment has occurred for him. It will then become definite and certain for him that he knows no sun and no earth, but always only an eye that sees the sun, a hand that feels the earth; that the world which surrounds him is there only as mental picture, i.e., that it absolutely is there only in relationship to something else, to the one doing the mental picturing, which he himself is.—If ever a truth could be declared a priori, it is this one; for it is the expression of that form which every possible and imaginable experience has, that form which is more general than all others, such as time, space, and causality; for all these already presuppose the

---

**Die Welt als Wille und Vorstellung* (usually translated *The World as Will and Representation*).

first form . . ." This whole thesis founders upon the fact
I have already indicated above, that the eye and the hand
are no less perceptions than the sun and the earth. And
one could, in Schopenhauer's sense and in his own terms,
confront his thesis with: My eye that sees the sun, and
my hand that feels the earth are my mental pictures in
just the same way as the sun and earth themselves are.
That I thereby invalidate his thesis, however, is immediately clear. For only my real eye and my real hand could
have, connected to them as their own modifications, the
mental pictures sun and earth; my mental pictures of eye
and hand could not however have these mental pictures.
But only of *these* can critical idealism speak.

Critical idealism is totally unfitted to gain a view of the
relationship between perception and mental picture. To
distinguish, as indicated on page 49, between what is
happening with the perception during the act of perceiving, and what must already be there in the perception
before it is perceived—this, critical idealism cannot under-
take to do. In order to do this, therefore, another path
must be taken.

V
The Activity of Knowing the World

It follows from the preceding considerations that it is impossible, through investigation of the content of our observation, to prove that our perceptions are mental pictures. This was supposedly proven by showing that if the process of perception does take place in the way one pictures it in accordance with the naive-realistic assumptions about the psychological and physiological constitution of our individuality, then we do not have to do with things-in-themselves, but merely with our mental pictures of the things. Now if naive realism, consistently pursued, leads to results which represent the exact opposite of its presuppositions, then these presuppositions must be deemed unfit for founding a world view and must be dropped. In any case it is inadmissible to reject the presuppositions and to allow what follows from them to hold good, as does the critical idealist, who bases his assertion that the world is my mental picture upon the line of argument above. (Eduard von Hartmann, in his book *The Basic Problem of Epistemology*, gives a detailed presentation of this line of argument.)

The correctness of critical idealism is one thing; the power of its proofs to convince is another. How matters stand with respect to the former will be shown later in the course of our considerations. But the power of its proof to convince is nil. If someone builds a house, and with the addition of the second floor, the ground floor collapses, the second floor falls along with it. Naive realism and critical idealism relate to each other as this ground floor to the second floor.

Whoever is of the view that the entire perceived world is only a mental picture, and indeed the effect upon my soul of things unknown to me, for him the real question of knowledge has to do of course not with the mental pictures which are only present in my soul, but rather with the things which lie beyond our consciousness and are independent of us. He asks how much we can know *indirectly* about the latter, since they are not *directly* accessible to our observation. Someone taking this standpoint does not bother himself about the inner connection of his conscious perceptions, but only about their no longer conscious causes, which have an existence independent of him, while, in his view, the perceptions disappear as soon as he turns his senses away from the things. Our consciousness functions, from this point of view, like a mirror, whose images of specific things also disappear the moment its reflecting surface is not directed toward them. Someone, however, who does not see the things themselves, but only their mirror images, must, from the behavior of the latter, inform himself indirectly by inferences about the nature of the former. This is the standpoint of modern science, which uses perceptions only as a last resort in order to obtain information about the processes of matter which stand behind our perceptions and which alone truly exist. If the philosopher as critical idealist allows any real being to exist at all, then his striving for knowledge, using mental pictures as a means, directs itself only to this real being. His interest skips over the subjective world of mental pictures and goes straight for what produces these mental pictures.

But the critical idealist can go so far as to say that I am closed off in my world of mental pictures and cannot get out of it. If I think a thing behind my mental pictures, this thought is also, after all, nothing more than my mental picture. Such an idealist will then either deny the thing-in-itself completely, or at least declare it to have absolutely no significance for human beings, which means that it is as good as not there, because we can know nothing about it.

To a critical idealist of this sort, the whole world appears as a dream, in the face of which any urge for knowledge would be simply meaningless. For him there can be only two types of people: deluded ones, who consider their own dream-spinnings to be real things, and wise ones, who see into the nothingness of this dream world and who, by and by, must lose all desire to bother themselves further about it. From this standpoint even one's own personality can become a mere dream image. In exactly the same way as our own dream image appears among the images of our sleep-dreams, the mental picture of my own "I" joins the mental picture of the outer world within waking consciousness. We are given in our consciousness then, not our real "I," but only our mental picture "I." Now, whoever denies that things exist, or at least denies that we can know anything about them, must also deny the existence—or, at least the knowledge—of his own personality. The critical idealist comes then to the declaration, "All reality transforms itself into a wonderful dream, without a life that is dreamt, and without a spirit who is having the dream; into a dream that hangs together with a dream about itself." (See Fichte, *The Vocation of Man.*★)

It does not matter whether the person who believes that he knows our immediate life to be a dream imagines there to be nothing behind this dream, or whether he relates his mental pictures to real things: life itself must lose all scientific interest for him. But while all science must be total nonsense for the person who believes that the universe accessible to us is limited to a dream, for the person who believes himself able to draw inferences about the things from his mental pictures, science will consist in investigating these "things-in-themselves." The first view can be called absolute *illusionism*; the second view is called *transcendental realism* by Eduard von Hartmann, its most consequential proponent.★★

Both these views have in common with naive realism that they seek to gain a footing in the world through an

---

★*Die Bestimmung des Menschen*

★★In the terms of this world view, knowledge is called *transcendental* which believes itself to be conscious of the fact that nothing can be directly stated about the things-in-themselves, but which draws indirect inferences, from the known subjective, about the unknown lying beyond the subjective (the transcendental). According to this view, the thing-in-itself is beyond the sphere of the world *directly* knowable for us: i.e., it is transcendent. Our world, however, can be related to the transcendental transcendentally. Hartmann's view is called realism, because it goes out beyond the subjective, the ideal, to the transcendental, the real.

investigation of perceptions. But within this realm they are nowhere able to find firm ground.

A major question for the proponent of transcendental realism would have to be how the "I" brings about the world of mental pictures out of itself. A serious striving for knowledge about a world of mental pictures given to us, which disappears as soon as we close our senses to the outer world, can kindle itself only to the extent that such a world is a means of investigating indirectly the world of the "I"-in-itself. If the things of our experience were mental pictures, then our everyday life would be like a dream and knowledge of the true state of affairs would be like waking up. Our dream pictures also interest us as long as we are dreaming and therefore not recognizing them in their dream character. The moment we wake up we no longer ask about the inner connections of our dream pictures, but rather about the physical, physiological, and psychological processes that underlie them. Just as little can the philosopher, who considers the world to be his mental picture, interest himself in the inner connections of the details of this world. If he admits to an existing "I" at all, he will not then ask how one of his mental pictures relates to another, but rather what occurs, within the soul existing independently of him, while his consciousness contains a certain train of mental pictures. If I dream that I am drinking wine which causes a burning in my throat, and then wake up with an irritation in my throat that makes me cough (see Weygandt, *How Dreams Arise*, 1893*), then, the moment I wake up, the dream event ceases to have an interest for me. My atten-

*Entstehung der Träume.

tion is now directed only toward the physiological and psychological processes through which the irritation in my throat brings itself symbolically to expression in the dream picture. In the same way, as soon as he is convinced that the world given him has the character of mental pictures, the philosopher must skip over this world into the real soul existing behind it. The situation is far worse, to be sure, if illusionism totally denies the ''I''-in-itself behind the mental pictures, or at least considers it to be unknowable. One can very easily be led to such a view by the observation that, in contrast to dreaming, there is indeed the waking state, in which we have the chance to see through our dreams and to relate them to real circumstances, but that we have no state which stands in a similar relationship to our life of waking consciousness. Whoever adopts this view lacks the insight that there is something which in fact does relate to mere perceiving in the same way that experience in the waking state relates to dreaming. This something is *thinking*.

The naive person cannot be accused of the lack of insight referred to here. He gives himself over to life and takes things as real in the form they present themselves to him in experience. But the first step which is undertaken to go beyond this standpoint can only consist in the question of how thinking relates to the perception. Regardless of whether or not the perception continues to exist in the form presented to me before and after my mental picturing: if I want to say anything at all about the perception, this can happen only with the help of thinking. If I say that the world is my mental picture, I have expressed thereby the result of a thought process, and if my thinking is not applicable to the world, then this result is an error. Between the perception and any kind of statement about it, thinking presses in.

We have already given the reason why, during the contemplation of things, thinking is for the most part overlooked (see page 28). The reason lies in the fact that we direct our attention only upon the object we are thinking about, but not at the same time upon our thinking. The naive consciousness therefore treats thinking as something which has nothing to do with the things, but which stands completely apart from them and carries on its contemplation of the world. The picture of the phenomena of the world that the thinker sketches is regarded, not as something which belongs to the things, but rather as something existing only in man's head; the world is also complete without this picture. The world is set and complete in all its substances and forces; and of this complete world man sketches a picture. One must only ask those who think in this way, what right they have to declare the world complete without thinking. Does not the world bring forth thinking in the head of man with the same necessity as it brings forth the blossom from the plant? Plant a seed in the earth. It puts forth root and stem. It opens into leaves and blossoms. Set the plant before you. It unites in your soul with a definite concept. Why does this concept belong any less to the whole plant than leaf and blossom do? You say that the leaves and blossoms are there without a perceiving subject; that the concept appears only when the human being stands before the plant. Quite so. But blossoms and leaves also arise on the plant only when earth is there, into which the seed can be placed, when light and air are there, within which leaves and blossoms can unfold. The concept of the plant arises in exactly the same way when a thinking consciousness approaches the plant.

It is entirely arbitrary to regard the sum of what we experience of a thing through mere perception as a totality, as a complete whole, and to regard what results from *thinking* contemplation as something merely added on which has nothing to do with the thing itself. If I am given a rosebud today, the picture presented to my perception is complete only for the moment. If I set the bud in water, then I will be given a completely different picture of my object tomorrow. If I do not turn my eye from the rosebud, then I will see its present stage pass over continuously into tomorrow's, through innumerable intermediary stages. The picture presented to me at any specific moment is only a chance part taken from an object that is continuously becoming. If I do not set the bud in water, then it will not bring to development a whole series of stages which lie in it as potential. Likewise I can be prevented from further observation of the blossom tomorrow, and thus have an incomplete picture.

It is a completely unfounded opinion, bound to chance happenings, which would declare, with reference to the picture presented at one particular time, that *that* is the thing.

Just as little is it admissible to declare that the sum total of a thing's perceptual characteristics is the thing. It could very well be possible that a spirit was able to receive the concept at the same time as, and unseparated from, the perception. It would not occur at all to such a spirit to regard the concept as something not belonging to the thing. He would have to ascribe to the concept an existence inseparably bound up with the thing.

Let me make myself even clearer through an example. If I throw a stone horizontally through the air, I see it in different places, one after another. I connect these places into a line. In mathematics I learn to know different line forms, among them the parabola. I know the parabola to be a line that arises when a point moves in a certain lawful way. When I investigate the conditions under which the thrown stone moves, I find that the line of its motion is identical with that which I know as a parabola. That the stone happens to move in a parabola is the result of the given conditions and follows necessarily from them. The form of the parabola belongs to the whole phenomenon just as much as everything else about it which comes into consideration. The spirit described above, who did not have to take the roundabout way of thinking, would not only be given a sum of sight sensations at different places, but also, unseparated from the phenomenon, the parabolic form of the trajectory, which *we* only then add to the phenomenon through thinking.

It is not due to the objects that they are given to us at first without their corresponding concepts, but rather it is due to our spiritual organization. Our total being functions in such a way that, for each thing within reality, the elements which come into consideration about the thing flow to us from two sides: from the sides of *perceiving* and of *thinking*.

How I am organized to grasp things has nothing to do with their nature. The split between perceiving and thinking is first present the moment I, the observing person, approach the things. Which elements do or do not belong to the thing cannot depend at all upon the way I arrive at knowledge about these elements.

Man is a limited being. First of all he is a being among other beings. His existence belongs to space and time. Because of this fact there only a limited part of the total universe can be given him. But this limited part connects on all sides, both in time and in space, with other things. Were our existence joined to things in such a way that every happening in the world would be at the same time *our* happening, then there would not be a distinction between us and things. But then there would also be no individual things for us. Then all happening would merge together into a continuum. The cosmos would be a unity and a self-enclosed whole. The flow of happening would be interrupted nowhere. Because of our limitation something appears to us as individual which is not in truth an individual thing. Nowhere, for example, is the individual quality of red present all by itself. It is surrounded on all sides by other qualities, to which it belongs, and without which it could not exist. For us, however, it is necessary to lift certain parts out of the world and to look at them in their own right. Our eye can grasp individual colors only one by one out of a complex of many colors; our intellect can grasp only individual concepts out of a system of interrelated concepts. This separating out is a subjective act, and is due to the fact that we are not identical with the world process, but are one being among other beings.

Everything depends now on determining the place of that being, which we ourselves are, in relationship to the other beings. This determination must be distinguished from the mere becoming conscious of ourselves. This last is based on the act of perceiving, just as is our becoming conscious of every other thing. The perception of myself shows me a sum of characteristics, which I bring together into my personality as a whole, in the same way that I bring together the characteristics of yellow, metallically-shiny, hard, etc., into the unity "gold." The perception of myself does not lead me out of the realm of what belongs to me. This perception of myself is to be distinguished from what I determine, *thinking*, about myself. Just as, through my thinking, I incorporate an individual perception of the outer world into the whole world complex, so do I incorporate the perceptions I have about myself into the world process through thinking. My perceiving of myself encloses me within definite limits; my thinking has nothing to do with these limits. In this sense I am a twofold being. I am enclosed within the region which I perceive as that of my personality, but I am the bearer of an activity which, from a higher sphere, determines my limited existence. Our thinking is not individual the way our experiencing and feeling are. It is universal. It receives an individual stamp in each single person only through the fact that it is related to his individual feeling and experiencing. Through these particular colorings of the universal thinking, individual people differ from one another. A triangle has only one single concept. For the content of this concept it is a matter of indifference whether the human bearer of consciousness who grasps it is A or B. But the content of this concept will be grasped in an individual way by each of the two bearers of consciousness.

This thought is opposed by a preconception people

have which is difficult to overcome. This bias does not attain to the insight that the concept of the triangle which my head grasps is the same as the one comprehended by the head of my neighbor. The naive person considers himself to be the creator of his concepts. He believes, therefore, that each person has his own concepts. It is a fundamental requirement of philosophical thinking that it overcome this preconception. The oneness of the concept "triangle" does not become a plurality through the fact that it is thought by many. For the thinking of the many is itself a oneness.

In thinking we have given to us the element which fuses our particular individuality into one whole with the cosmos. Inasmuch as we experience and feel (and also perceive), we are separate beings; inasmuch as we think, we are the all-one being, which permeates all. This is the deeper basis of our twofold nature: we see an utterly absolute power come into existence within us, a power which is universal; but we learn to know it, not where it streams forth from the center of the world, but rather at a point on the periphery. If the first were the case, then the moment we came to consciousness, we would know the solution to the whole riddle of the world. Since we stand at a point on the periphery, however, and find our own existence enclosed within certain limits, we must learn to know the region which lies outside of our own being with the help of thinking, which projects into us out of the general world existence.

Through the fact that the thinking in us reaches out beyond our separate existence and relates itself to universal existence, there arises in us the drive for knowledge.

Beings without thinking do not have this drive. When other things confront them, no questions are aroused thereby. These other things remain external to such beings. With thinking beings, when confronted by an outer thing, the concept wells up. The concept is what we receive from the thing, not from without, but rather from within. *Knowledge* is meant to yield the balance, the union of the two elements, the inner and the outer.

A perception* is therefore nothing finished, closed off, but rather it is the one side of total reality. The other side is the concept. The act of knowledge is the synthesis of perception and concept. The perception and the concept of a thing, however, first constitute the entire thing.

The preceding considerations yield proof that it is nonsensical to seek something which the individual entities of the world have in common beyond the ideal content with which thinking presents us. All attempts must founder which strive for any world unity other than this self-coherent ideal content which we acquire for ourselves through thinking contemplation of our perceptions. Not a human personal God, not force or matter, nor will without idea (Schopenhauer) can be considered by us to be a valid universal world unity. These beings all belong to only one limited region of our observation. Humanly limited personality we perceive only with respect to ourselves, force and matter only with respect to outer things. With respect to the will, it can only be considered to be what our limited personality manifests as activity. Schopen-

*By "perception" Rudolf Steiner still means the *object* of perception, not the act of perceiving. See pages 32–34.—Translator's note.

hauer wants to avoid making "abstract" thinking into
the bearer of world unity, and seeks, instead of it, something which presents itself to him directly as real. This
philosopher believes that we will never really get at the
world as long as we regard it as an outer world. "In actuality, the sought-for meaning of the world which confronts me solely as my mental picture, or the transition
from this world, as mere mental picture of the subject
knowing it, over to what it might still be besides mental
picture, could nevermore be found, if the researcher himself were nothing more than purely knowing subject (winged
angel's head without body). But now he himself has roots
in that world, finds himself in it, namely, as an *individual*, which means that his activity of knowing, which
is the determining bearer of the whole world as a mental
picture, is after all given entirely through the medium of
a body, whose sensations, as shown, are the starting point
for the intellect in viewing that world. For the purely
knowing subject as such, this body is a mental picture
like any other, an object among objects: the motions, the
actions of it are known to him in that respect no differently than the changes in all other observable objects, and
would be just as foreign and incomprehensible to him, if
the significance of his own motions and actions were not
disclosed to him somehow in a completely different way.
. . . To the knowing subject, which arises as an individual
through its identification with the body, this body is
given in two completely different ways: one is as a mental
picture when the body is viewed intellectually, as object
among objects, and subject to the laws of these objects;
but then at the same time in a completely different way

also as that something, known directly by everyone, which the word *"will"* characterizes. Every true act of his will is immediately and unfailingly also a movement of his body: he cannot really will an act, without at the same time perceiving that it manifests as a movement of his body. The act of will and the action of the body are not two objectively known different states, connected by the bond of causality; they do not stand in the relationship of cause and effect; but they are rather one and the same, only given in two completely different ways: one completely direct and one for the intellect in contemplation." By this train of thought Schopenhauer believes himself justified in finding the *objectivity* of will within the human body. He is of the opinion that, in the actions of the body, he feels *directly* a reality, the thing-in-itself in concreto. Against these arguments it must be objected that the actions of our body come to consciousness only through self-perceptions and as such have nothing over other perceptions. If we want to *know* their nature, we can do this only through *thinking* contemplation, that means through incorporating them into the ideal system of our concepts and ideas.

Most deeply rooted in the naive consciousness of mankind is the opinion that thinking is abstract, without any concrete content. It can give at most an "ideal" reflection of the world whole, but definitely not this world whole itself. Whoever judges in this way has never made clear to himself what a perception is without its concept. But let us look at this world of perception: it appears as mere juxtaposition in space and succession in time, an aggregate of particulars without interconnection. Not one of the things which come and go there upon the stage of perception has anything, which can be perceived, to do directly with any other. There, the world is a multiplicity of objects of equal value. None plays a role greater than any other in the functioning of the world. If we want to become clear about whether this or that fact has greater significance than the other, then we must consult our thinking. If our thinking is not working, we see an animal's rudimentary organ, which has no significance for its life, as of equal value with its most important bodily member. The individual facts come forth in their significance, both for themselves and with respect to the other parts of the world, only when thinking weaves its threads from being to being. This activity of thinking is one *full of content*. For only through an altogether definite and concrete content can I know why the snail stands at a lower stage of development than does the lion. Mere sight, mere perception gives me no content which could instruct me as to the level of organization.

Thinking, out of man's world of concepts and ideas, brings this content to meet the perception. In contrast to the content of perception, which is given us from outside, the content of thought appears within us. Let us call the form in which it first arises, *"intuition."* Intuition is for thinking what *observation* is for the perception. Intuition and observation are the sources of our knowledge. We confront an observed thing in the world as foreign to us, as long as we do not have within us the corresponding intuition which fills in the piece of reality missing in the perception. For someone who does not have the ability to find the intuitions which correspond to the things, full reality remains closed. Just as the colorblind person sees only differences in brightness without the qualities of color, so the person without intuition can only observe unconnected perceptual fragments.

To explain a thing, *to make it comprehensible,* means nothing other than to set it into the context out of which it has been torn through the configuration of our organization described above. There is no such thing as an object separated off from the whole world. All separating off has only subjective validity for our organization. For us the whole world breaks down into above and below, before and after, cause and effect, thing and mental picture, matter and force, object and subject, etc. The single things which confront us in observation join themselves together, part by part, through the interconnected, unified world of our intuitions; and through thinking we join together again into oneness everything which we have separated through our perceiving.

The puzzling aspect of an object lies in its separate existence. This puzzling aspect, however, is evoked by us, and can, within the conceptual world, also be dispelled again.

Other than through thinking and perceiving, nothing is given us directly. The question now arises as to how things stand, in the light of these considerations, with respect to the significance of the perception. We have, to be sure, recognized that the proof which critical idealism brings of the subjective nature of our perceptions collapses; but along with this insight into the incorrectness of its proof, it is still not yet determined that the view itself is based on error. Critical idealism, in marshalling its proof, does not take its start from the absolute nature of thinking, but rather bases itself upon the fact that naive realism, consistently pursued, cancels itself out. How does the matter present itself if the absoluteness of thinking is recognized?

Let us assume that a certain perception, red for example, arises in my consciousness. The perception shows itself, as I continue looking, to be connected with other perceptions, for example with that of a certain shape, with certain temperature and tactile perceptions. This combination I designate as an object of the sense world. I can now ask myself what else is to be found, besides this object, in that section of space within which the above perceptions appear to me. I will find mechanical, chemical, and other processes within this part of space. Now I go further and investigate the processes that I find on the way from the object to my sense organ. I can find processes of motion within an elastic medium, which, by their very nature, do not have the least thing in common with the original perceptions. I get the same result when I investigate the further transmitting from sense organ to brain. In each of these areas I have new perceptions; but what weaves as a connecting medium through all these spatially and temporally separated perceptions is thinking. The vibrations of the air which transmit the sound are given to me as perceptions in exactly the same way as the sound itself. Only thinking joins all these perceptions to each other and reveals them in their mutual interrelationships. We cannot say that anything other than what is directly perceived exists except what is known through the ideal interconnections of our perceptions (ideal in that they are to be discovered through thinking). The relationship, going beyond what is merely perceived, of the object of perception to the subject of perception, is therefore a purely ideal one, that means, expressible only through concepts. Only in the event that I could perceive how the object of perception affects the subject of perception, or, the other way round, that I could observe the building up of the perceptible entity by the subject, would it be possible to speak as does modern physiology and the critical idealism founded upon it. This view confuses an ideal relationship (of the object to the subject) with a process which could only be spoken of if it were perceivable. The sentence: "No color without a color-sensitive eye," therefore cannot mean that the eye brings forth the color, but rather only that an ideal connection, knowable through thinking, exists between the perception "color" and the perception "eye." Empirical science will have to determine how the characteristics of the eye and those of colors relate to each other; through which configurations the organ of sight transmits the perception of colors, etc. I can follow how one perception follows upon another, how it stands spatially in relationship with other perceptions; and I can bring this then into a conceptual formulation; but I cannot perceive how a perception comes forth out of the unperceivable. All endeavors to seek relationships between perceptions other than thought relationships must necessarily founder.

What, then, is a perception? This question, when asked in a general way, is absurd. A perception always arises as an entirely specific one, as a definite content. This content is directly given, and is all that is in the given. One can only ask with respect to this given, what it is besides perception, i.e., what it is for thinking. Thus, the question about the "what" of a perception can only refer to the conceptual intuition that corresponds to it. From this point of view the question as to the subjectivity of the perception in the sense of critical idealism cannot be raised at all. Only that may be labeled as subjective which is perceived as belonging to the subject. To form the bond between subjective and objective is not the task of any real process in the naive sense, i.e. of any perceptible happening; rather, it is the task of thinking alone. For us, therefore, something is objective which presents itself to perception as situated outside of the perceiving subject. My perceiving subject remains perceptible to me when the table now standing in front of me will have disappeared from the circle of my observation. The observation of the table has called forth in me a change, which likewise remains. I retain the ability to create a picture of the table again later. This ability to bring forth a picture remains connected with me. Psychology calls this picture a memory picture. It is, however, that which alone can rightly be called the *mental picture* of the table. This picture corresponds, namely, to the perceptible change of my own state through the presence of the table within my field of vision. And indeed, this change does not refer to any "I-in-itself" standing behind the perceiving subject, but rather the change of the perceptible subject himself. The mental picture is therefore a subjective perception in contrast to the objective perception when the object is present on the horizon of perception. The confusing of the subjective with the objective perception leads to the mistaken view of idealism: that the world is my mental picture.

It will now be our next task to determine more closely the concept of the mental picture. What we have brought forward so far about the mental picture is not its concept, but only indicates the path along which it is to be found within the field of perception. The exact concept of the mental picture will then also make it possible for us to gain a satisfactory explanation of the relationship of mental picture and object. This will then also lead us over the boundary where the relationship between human subject and the object belonging to the world will be led down from the purely conceptual field of knowing activity into our concrete individual *life*. Once we know what to make of the world, it will be an easy matter also to orient ourselves accordingly. We can be active with our full strength only when we know the object, belonging to the world, to which we are devoting our activity.

Addendum to the Revised Edition of 1918. The view characterized here can be regarded as one to which man is at first as though naturally impelled when he begins to reflect upon his relationship to the world. He seems himself entangled in a thought configuration which unravels for him as he is forming it. This thought configuration is of such a kind that everything necessary for it is not yet fulfilled with its merely theoretical refutation. One must *live it through* in order, out of insight into the aberration into which it leads, to find the way out. It must appear within an investigation of the relationship of man to the world, not because one wants to refute others whom one believes to hold an incorrect view about this relationship, but rather because one must know what perplexity every first reflection upon such a relationship can bring. One must gain *the* insight as to how one can refute *oneself* with respect to these first reflections. This is the point of view from which the above line of argumentation is put forward.

Whoever wants to develop for himself a view about the relationship of man to the world becomes conscious that he brings about at least a part of this relationship through the fact that he makes mental pictures for himself about the things and occurrences of the world. Through this, his gaze is drawn away from what is *outside* in the world and directed upon his inner world, upon his life of mental pictures. He begins to say to himself, "I can have a relationship to no thing and to no occurrence, if a mental picture does not arise in me." From noting this fact, it is only a step to the opinion that I do, after all, experience only my mental pictures; I know of a world outside of me only insofar as it is a mental picture *within me*. With this opinion the naive standpoint of reality is abandoned which the human being takes before any reflecting about his relationship to the world. From this standpoint, he believes he has to do with real things. Self-reflection forces him away from this standpoint. It does not let him look at all upon a reality such as naive consciousness believes to have before itself. It lets him look merely upon his mental pictures; *these* interpose themselves between one's own being and a supposed real world such as the naive standpoint believes itself justified in affirming. The human being can no longer look, through the intervening world of mental images, upon a reality such as that. He must assume that he is blind to this reality. In this way there arises the thought of a "thing-in-itself" which is inaccessible to knowledge.—So long as one goes no further than to contemplate the relationship to the world into which man seems to enter through his life of mental pictures, one will not be able to escape this thought configuration. One cannot remain at the naive standpoint of reality if one does not want to close oneself off artificially to the desire for knowledge. The fact that this desire for knowledge about the relationship of man and world is present, shows that this naive standpoint must be abandoned. If the naive standpoint offered something which one can acknowledge as the truth, then one could not feel this desire.—But one does not arrive at something different which one could regard as the truth, if one merely abandons the naive standpoint, but—without noticing it—retains the kind of thinking which this standpoint imposes. One falls into just such an error when one says to oneself, "I experience only my mental pictures, and although I believe that I am dealing with realities, I am only conscious of my mental pictures of realities; I must therefore assume that only outside of the circle of my consciousness do the true realities, the 'things-in-themselves,' lie, of which I know absolutely nothing directly, which somehow approach me and influence me in such a way that my world of mental pictures arises in me." Whoever thinks in this way only adds in thought, to the world lying before him, another one; but, with respect to this world, he would actually have to start all over again from the beginning with his thought work. For the unknown "thing-in-itself" is thereby thought to be no different at all in its relationship to man's own being than the known thing of the naive standpoint of reality.—One escapes the perplexity into which one comes through pondering this standpoint critically only when one notices that there is something—*within* what a person can experience and perceive inside himself and outside in the world—that absolutely cannot suffer the fate of having the mental picture interpose itself between the occurrence and the contemplating human being. And *this* is *thinking*. With respect to thinking, the human being *can* remain upon the naive standpoint towards reality. If he does not do so, it is only because he has noticed that for something else he must abandon this standpoint, but does not become aware that the insight thus gained is not applicable to thinking. If he becomes aware of this, then he opens the way for himself to the other insight, that *within* thinking and *through* thinking, he must come to know that element to which man seems to blind himself through the fact that he must interpose his life of mental pictures between the world and himself.—The author of this book has been reproached by someone highly esteemed by him for remaining, in his consideration of thinking, at a naive realism of thinking like the sort which exists when one regards the real world and the mentally pictured world as one. But the author of these considerations believes that he has in fact shown that the validity of this "naive realism" *for thinking* does necessarily follow out of an unprejudiced observation of thinking; and that the naive realism which is otherwise not valid is overcome through the knowledge of the true being of thinking.

VI
The Human Individuality

The main difficulty in explaining mental pictures is found by philosophers to lie in the fact that we are not ourselves the outer things, and yet our mental pictures must still have a form corresponding to the things. On closer examination, however, it turns out that this difficulty does not exist at all. We are not, to be sure, the outer things, but we belong, with the outer things, to one and the same world. The section of the world that I perceive as my subject is swept through by the stream of general world happening. To my perception I am at first enclosed within the boundary of my skin. But what is present there inside this skin belongs to the cosmos as a whole. Therefore, in order for a connection to exist between my organism and the object outside me, it is not necessary at all that something of the object slip into me or make an imprint in my spirit like a signet ring in wax. The question as to how I take cognizance of the tree that stands ten steps distant from me, is all askew. It springs from the view that the boundaries of my body are absolute barriers, through which information about the things wanders into me. The forces which are at work inside my skin are the same ones as those existing outside it. I am, therefore, really the things; not I, to be sure, insofar as I am the perceiving subject, but I, insofar as I am a part within general world happening. My perception of the tree exists within the same whole as does my "I." This general world happening calls forth just as much there the perception of the tree as here the perception of my "I." If I were not a world knower, but rather a world creator, then object and subject (perception and "I"), would originate in one act. For they determine each other mutually. As world knower, I can find what both have in common—as two sides of one existence which belong together—only through thinking, which relates both to each other through concepts.

Most difficult to drive from the field will be the so-called physiological proofs for the subjectivity of our perceptions. If I exert pressure on my skin, I perceive it as a sensation of pressure. I can perceive the same pressure through the eye as light, and through the ear as sound. I perceive an electrical discharge through the eye as light, through the ear as sound, through the nerves of the skin as impact, through the nose as a phosphoric smell. What follows from this fact? Only this, that I perceive an electrical discharge (or a pressure) and then a certain quality of light, or a sound, perhaps a certain smell, and so on. If no eye were there, then the perception of a light quality would not accompany the perception of a mechanical concussion in the environment; without the presence of an organ of hearing, no perception of sound, and so on. By what right can one say that without organs of perception the whole process would not be present? Whoever concludes from the fact that an electrical process calls forth light in the eye that therefore what we experience as light is, outside of our organism, only a mechanical process of motion—he forgets that he is only passing from one perception to another, and not at all to something outside of perception. Just as one can say that the eye perceives a mechanical process of motion in its environment as light, one can just as well maintain that changing an object in an ordered way is perceived by us as a process of motion. If I paint a horse twelve times all the way around a rotatable disk, in exactly those forms which his body would assume if he were running along, then, through rotating the disk I can call forth an appearance of motion. I only need to look through an opening in such a way as to see, at the right intervals, the sequence of the horses' positions. I do not see twelve pictures of a horse, but rather the picture of a galloping horse.

The physiological fact mentioned above can therefore throw no light on the relationship between perception and mental picture. We must find our right course in a different way.

The moment a perception rises up on the horizon of my observation, thinking also becomes active through me. An entity within my system of thoughts, a particular intuition, a concept, joins itself to the perception. When the perception then disappears from my field of vision, what remains? My intuition—with its connection to the particular perception—which formed at the moment of perceiving. The liveliness with which I can then later make this connection present to myself again, depends upon the way my spiritual and bodily organism functions. The *mental picture* is nothing other than an intuition related to a particular perception, a concept which was once connected to a perception, and for which the relation to this perception has remained. My concept of a lion is not formed *out of* my perceptions of lions. But my mental picture of a lion is very much formed *from* perception. I can convey the concept of a lion to someone who has never seen a lion. But I will not succeed in conveying to him a lively mental picture without his own perception. The *mental picture* is therefore an individualized concept. And now we have the explanation as to why the things of the real world can be represented for us through mental pictures. The full reality of a thing yields itself to us at the moment of observation out of the coming together of concept and perception. The concept receives, through a perception, an individual form, a relation to this particular perception. In this individual form, which bears within itself as a characteristic feature the relation to the perception, the concept lives on within us and constitutes the mental picture of the thing in question. If we meet a second thing, with which the same concept connects itself, we then recognize it as belonging, with the first thing, to the same kind; if we meet the same thing again a second time, we find within our system of concepts not only a corresponding concept, but also the individualized concept with its characteristic relation to the same object, and we recognize the object again.

The mental picture stands therefore between perception and concept. It is the particular concept pointing to the perception.

The sum of that about which I can form mental pictures I may call my experience. That person will have the richer experience who has a greater number of individualized concepts. A person who lacks any capacity for intuitions is not capable of acquiring experience for himself. He loses the objects again from his field of vision, because he lacks the concepts which he should bring into relation with them. A person with a well-developed ability to think, but with poorly functioning perception because of dull sense organs, will be equally unable to gather experience. He can, it is true, acquire concepts in one way or another; but his intuitions lack the living relationship to particular things. The unthinking traveler and the scholar living in abstract conceptual systems are equally unable to acquire a rich experience for themselves.

Reality presents itself to us as perception and concept; our subjective representation of this reality presents itself to us as mental picture.

If our personality manifested itself merely as knower, then the sum of everything objective would be given in perception, concept, and mental picture.

We are not content, however, to relate, with the help of thinking, the perception to the concept, but we also relate it to our particular subjectivity, to our individual "I." The expression of this individual relationship is feeling, which has its life in pleasure or pain.

Thinking and *feeling* correspond to the twofold nature of our being upon which we have already reflected. *Thinking* is the element through which we participate in the general happening of the cosmos; *feeling* is that through which we can draw ourselves back into the confines of our own being.

Our thinking unites us with the world; our feeling leads

us back into ourselves, first makes us into an individual. If we were merely thinking and perceiving beings, our whole life would have to flow along in unvarying indifference. If we could merely *know* ourselves as self, we would be completely indifferent to ourselves. Only through the fact that we experience a feeling of self along with self-knowledge, and pleasure and pain along with our perception of things, do we live as individual beings, whose existence is not limited to the conceptual relationship in which they stand to the rest of the world, but who also have a particular value for themselves.

One might be tempted to see in the life of feeling an element that is more richly saturated with reality than is our thinking contemplation of the world. The reply to this is that it is only for my individuality, in fact, that my life of feeling has this richer significance. For the world as a whole, my life of feeling can achieve any value only when my feeling, as a perception made about my self, unites itself with a concept, and in this roundabout way members itself into the cosmos.

Our life is a continuous swing of the pendulum between our life in general world happening and our own individual existence. The farther we ascend into the general nature of thinking, where what is individual still interests us only as example, as one instance of the concept, the more there is lost in us the character of our being a particular entity, an altogether specific single personality. The farther we descend into the depths of our own life and let our feelings sound along with our experiences of the outer world, the more we separate ourselves from universal existence. A true individuality will be the one who reaches up the farthest with his feelings into the region of the ideal. There are people with whom even the most general ideas that settle in their heads still bear that particular coloring which shows them to be unmistakably connected with their bearer. Other people exist whose concepts approach us without any trace of individual character, as though they had not sprung forth at all from a person of flesh and blood.

Our mental picturing already gives our life of concepts an individual stamp. Every person has, after all, his own place in the world where he stands and from which he contemplates the world. His concepts unite themselves with his perceptions. He will think universal concepts after his own fashion. This particular determining factor is a result of the place where we stand in the world, of the sphere of perception that is connected to our place in life.

Over against this determining factor there stands another one, which is dependent upon our particular organization. Our organization is, after all, a specific, fully determined entity. Each of us unites particular feelings— and this, indeed, with the most varying degrees of intensity—with his perceptions. This is what is individual about our own personality. It still remains as what is left when we have taken into account the determining factors of our place in life.

A life of feeling completely devoid of thought would gradually have to lose all connection with the world. Knowledge of things, for the person who cares about totality, will go hand in hand with the cultivation and development of his life of feeling.

Feeling is the means by which concepts first gain concrete *life*.

VII
Are There Limits to Knowing?

We have established that the elements needed for the explanation of reality are to be taken from the two spheres: perceiving and thinking. As we have seen, it is because of our organization that full, total reality, including our own subject, appears to us at first as a duality. The activity of knowing overcomes this duality inasmuch as, out of the two elements of reality—i.e., out of the perception and out of the concept produced by thinking—it joins together the complete thing. Let us call the way in which the world approaches us, before it has gained its rightful form through our knowing activity, "the world of appearance" in contrast to the entity composed, in a unified way, of perception and concept. Then we may say that the world is given us as a duality (dualistic), and our activity of knowing elaborates it into a unity (monistic). A philosophy which takes its starting point from this basic principle may be designated as a monistic philosophy or *monism*. Confronting this view there stands the two-world theory or *dualism*. This latter assumes, not just two sides of one unified reality, merely kept apart by our organization, but rather two worlds absolutely different from each other. It then seeks principles of explanation for one of these worlds within the other.

Dualism is based on an incorrect understanding of what we call knowledge. It separates the whole of existence into two regions, each of which has its own laws, and lets these regions stand over against one another outwardly.

Out of such a dualism has sprung the differentiation between the object of perception and the "thing-in-itself" which, through Kant, has been introduced into science and to the present day has not been expelled from it. According to our expositions, it lies in the nature of our spiritual organization that a particular thing can be given only as a perception. Our thinking then overcomes the separateness of the thing by assigning to each perception its lawful place within the world whole. As long as the separated parts of the world whole are designated as perceptions, we are simply following, in this separating out, a law of our subjectivity. But if we consider the sum total of all perceptions to be one part, and then place over against this part a second one in the "things-in-themselves," we are philosophizing off into the blue. Then we are merely playing with concepts. We are constructing an artificial polarity, but cannot gain any content for the second part of it, because such a content for a particular thing can be drawn only from perception.

Any kind of existence which is assumed outside the region of perception and concept is to be assigned to the sphere of unjustified hypotheses. The "thing-in-itself" belongs in this category. It is of course completely natural that the dualistic thinker cannot find the connection between his hypothetically assumed world principle and what is given in an experienceable way. A content for his hypothetical world principle can be gained only if one borrows it from the world of experience and deceives oneself about so doing. Otherwise his hypothetical world principle remains a concept devoid of any content, a nonconcept which only has the form of a concept. The dualistic thinker usually asserts then that the content of this concept is inaccessible to our knowledge; we can only know *that* such a content is present, not *what* is present. In both cases the overcoming of dualism is impossible. If one brings a few abstract elements from the world of experience into the concept of the thing-in-itself, it still remains impossible, in spite of this, to reduce the rich concrete life of experience down to a few characteristics which themselves are only taken from this perception. Du Bois-Reymond thinks that the unperceivable atoms of matter, through their position and motion, produce sensation and feeling, and then comes to the conclusion that we can never arrive at a satisfactory explanation as to how matter and motion produce sensation and feeling, for "it is, indeed, thoroughly and forever incomprehensible that it should not be a matter of indifference to a number of atoms of carbon, hydrogen, nitrogen, oxygen, etc. how they lie and move, how they lay and moved, how they will lie and move. There is no way to understand how consciousness could arise out of their interaction." This conclusion is characteristic for this whole trend of thought. Out of the rich world of perceptions are isolated: position and motion. These are carried over and applied to the imagined world of atoms. Then astonishment sets in about the fact that one cannot unfold concrete life out of this principle, which one has made oneself and which is borrowed from the world of perception.

That the dualist, working with a concept which is completely devoid of any content, of "in-itself," can come to no elucidation of the world, follows already from the definition of his principle presented above.

In any case, the dualist sees himself compelled to set insurmountable barriers before our ability to know. The adherent of a monistic world view knows that everything he needs to explain any given phenomenon of the world must lie within the sphere of this phenomenon given him. What might hinder him from attaining this explanation can only be barriers or shortcomings of his organization which chance to be there because of his time or place. And these are, in fact, not barriers and shortcomings of the human organization in general, but only of his particular individual one.

It follows from the concept of the activity of knowing, as we have determined this concept to be, that limits to knowledge cannot be spoken of. The activity of knowing is not a general concern of the world, but rather is a business which the human being has to settle with himself. Things demand no explanation. They exist and affect each other according to the laws which are discoverable through thinking. They exist in inseparable oneness with these laws. Our selfhood approaches the things then, and at first grasps only that part of them which we have called perception. But within the inner being of this selfhood, the power is to be found with which to find also the other part of reality. Only when my selfhood has united, also for itself, the two elements of reality which in the world are inseparably joined, is the satisfaction of knowledge then present: the "I" has attained reality again.

The preconditions for the coming into existence of the activity of knowing are therefore *through* and *for* the "I." The latter poses for itself the questions of knowing activity. And my "I" takes them, in fact, from the element of thinking, which is entirely clear and transparent in itself. If we pose ourselves questions which we cannot answer, then the content of the question must not be clear and definite in all its parts. It is not the world which poses us questions, but rather we ourselves who pose them.

I can imagine that I would lack any possibility of answering a question that I found written down somewhere, without knowing from which sphere the content of the question has been taken.

Our knowledge is concerned with questions that are posed us through the fact that, over against a sphere of perception which is determined by place, time, and my subjective organization, there stands a conceptual sphere which points to the totality of the world. My task consists in reconciling these two spheres, both well known to me, with each other. A limit to knowledge cannot be spoken of here. This or that can at some time or other remain unexplained because we are hindered by our place in life from perceiving the things that are at work there. What is not found today, however, can be found tomorrow. The barriers erected in this way are only transitory ones, which, with the progress of perception and thinking, can be overcome.

Dualism makes the mistake of transferring the antithesis of object and subject, which has significance only within the realm of perception, onto purely imaginary entities outside the realm of perception. But since the things, which are separated within the horizon of perception, are separate from each other only as long as the perceiving person refrains from thinking, which removes all separation and lets it be known as a merely subjectively determined one, the dualist transfers onto entities behind our perceptions characteristics which, even for these perceptions, have no absolute validity, but only a relative one. He thereby divides the two factors which come into consideration for the process of knowledge, perception and concept, into four: 1. the object-in-itself; 2. the perception which the subject has of the object; 3. the subject; 4. the concept which relates the perception to the object-in-itself. The relation between the object and subject is a *real* one; the subject is really (dynamically) influenced by the object. The real process is said not to fall within our consciousness. This real process, however, is said to evoke in the subject a countereffect to the effect coming from the object. The result of this countereffect is said to be the perception. This is what first falls within our consciousness. The object is said to have an objective reality (independent of the subject), the perception a subjective reality. This subjective reality is said to relate the subject to the object. This latter relation is said to be an ideal one. Dualism thus splits the process of knowledge into two parts. The one part, creation of the object of perception out of the "thing-in-itself," dualism lets take place *outside* our consciousness; the other part, connection of the perception with the concept and the relation of the concept to the object, dualism lets take place *inside our consciousness.* With these presuppositions it is clear that the dualist believes he can gain in his concepts only subjective representations of what lies *in front of* his consciousness. The objectively real process in the subject, through which the perception comes about, and all the more so, the objective interrelationships of the "things-in-themselves," remain unknowable in any direct way for such a dualist; in his opinion the human being can only create for himself conceptual representations of what is objectively real. The bond of unity among things, which joins these things with one another and objectively with our individual spirit (as "thing-in-itself"), lies beyond our consciousness in an existence-in-itself of which we would likewise only be able to have a conceptual representation within our consciousness.

Dualism believes it would rarify the whole world into an abstract conceptual pattern if it did not affirm, besides the conceptual relationships of objects, real relationships as well. In other words, the ideal principles to be found through thinking appear to the dualist to be too airy, and he seeks in addition to them real principles by which they can be supported.

Let us take a closer look at these real principles. The naive person (naive realist) regards the objects of outer experience as realities. The fact that he can grasp these things with his hands and see them with his eyes, is for him valid proof of their reality. "Nothing exists that one cannot perceive" is to be regarded as precisely the first axiom of the naive person, and it is accepted just as much in its reverse form: "Everything that can be perceived, exists.'' The best proof for this assertion is the naive person's belief in immortality and spirits. He pictures the soul to himself as fine physical matter, which under particular conditions can become visible, even to the ordinary person (naive belief in ghosts).

Compared to his real world, everything else for the naive realist, particularly the world of ideas, is unreal, "merely ideal.'' What we bring to the objects in thinking, that is mere thought *about* things. Our thought adds nothing real to our perception.

However, not only with respect to the existence of things does the naive person consider sense perception to be the only testimony of reality, but also with respect to processes. A thing can, in his view, only work upon another when a force present to sense perception goes forth from the one thing and lays hold of the other. Earlier physics believed that extremely fine substances stream out of material bodies and penetrate through our sense organs into the soul. The actual seeing of these substances is impossible only because of the coarseness of our senses compared with the fineness of these substances. In principle one granted reality to these substances for the same reason one grants it to the objects of the sense world, namely, because of their form of existence which was thought to be analogous to that of sense-perceptible reality.

The self-sustained being of what is ideally experienceable is not regarded by the naive consciousness as real in the same sense as what is experienceable by the senses. An object grasped in a "mere idea" is regarded as a mere chimera until conviction as to its reality can be given through sense perception. The naive person demands, to put it briefly, in addition to the ideal testimony of his thinking, the real testimony of his senses as well. In this need of the naive person lies the basis for the rise of the primitive forms of belief in revelation. The God who is given through thinking remains, to the naive consciousness, always a God who is only "*thought*." The naive consciousness demands a manifestation through means which are accessible to sense perception. God must appear in bodily form, and one wants to attach little value to the testimony of thinking but only to such things as proof of divinity through changing water into wine, which is verifiable by sense perception.

The naive person also pictures the activity of knowing as an occurrence analogous to the sense processes. The things make an *impression* in the soul, or they send out pictures which penetrate through the senses, and so on.

That which the naive person can perceive with his senses, he regards as real, and that of which he has no perception (God, soul, knowing, etc.), he pictures to himself as analogous to what is perceived.

If naive realism wants to found a science, it can view such a science only as the exact *description* of the content of perception. Concepts are for it only means to an end. They are there in order to create ideal reflections of our perceptions. For the things themselves they mean nothing. The naive realist regards as real only the individual tulips which are seen, or can be seen; he regards the one idea of tulip as an abstraction, as the unreal thought picture which the soul has composed for itself out of the features which all tulips have in common.

Experience, which teaches us that the content of our perceptions is of a transitory nature, refutes naive realism and its basic principle that everything which is perceived is real. The tulip that I see is real today; in a year it will have vanished into nothingness. What has maintained itself is the *species* tulip. But this species, for naive realism is *"only"* an *idea*, not a reality. Thus this world view finds itself in the situation of seeing its realities come and then vanish, while what it holds to be unreal maintains itself in the face of what is real. Therefore the naive realist must also allow, besides his perceptions, something else of an ideal nature to play its part. He must take up into himself entities which he cannot perceive with his senses. He comes to terms with this in that he thinks the form of existence of these entities to be analogous to that of sense objects. Such hypothetically assumed realities are the invisible forces through which sense–perceptible things act upon each other. One such thing is heredity, which transcends the individual, and which is the reason why, out of one individual, a new one develops, similar to it, through which the species maintains itself. Another such thing is the life principle permeating the bodily organism; another is the soul, for which the person of naive consciousness always finds a concept analogous to sense realities; and still another, finally, is the Divine Being of the naive person. This Divine Being is thought to be active in a way that corresponds exactly to what can be *perceived* of how the human being himself is active: anthropomorphically.

Modern physics traces sense impressions back to processes of the smallest parts of bodies and of an infinitely fine substance, of ether, or to something similar. What we, for example, experience as warmth is the motion of a body's parts within the space taken up by the body causing the warmth. Here also something unperceivable is again thought of as analogous to what is perceivable. The sense-perceptible analogy to the concept "body" is in this sense something like the interior of a space enclosed on all sides, within which elastic balls are moving in all directions, striking each other, bouncing on and off the walls and so on.

Without such assumptions the world would disintegrate for naive realism into an incoherent aggregate of perceptions without mutual relationships, that comes together in no kind of unity. It is clear, however, that naive realism can only come to this assumption through an inconsistency. If it wants to remain true to its basic principle that only what is perceived is real, then it ought not, after all, assume something real where it perceives nothing. The unperceivable forces which emanate from perceivable things are actually unjustified hypotheses from the standpoint of naive realism. And because it knows of no other realities, it endows its hypothetical forces with perceptible content. It therefore applies one form of being (that of perceptible existence) to a region where it lacks the means which alone has anything to say about this form of being: sense perception.

This self-contradictory world view leads to metaphysical realism. This constructs, besides perceivable reality, still another unperceivable one, which it thinks of as analogous to the first. Metaphysical realism is therefore necessarily dualism.

Wherever metaphysical realism notices a relationship

between perceivable things (movement toward something, becoming aware of something objective, and so on), there it postulates a reality. But the relationship which it notices, it can express only through thinking; it cannot perceive the relationship. The ideal relationship is arbitrarily made into something similar to what is perceivable. So for this trend of thought, the real world is composed of the objects of perception, which are in eternal becoming, which come and then vanish, and of the unperceivable forces by which the objects of perception are brought forth and which are what endure.

Metaphysical realism is a contradictory mixture of naive realism and idealism. Its hypothetical forces are unperceivable entities with the qualities of perceptions. It has decided—besides the region of the world for whose form of existence it has a means of knowledge in perception—to allow yet another region to exist, where this means fails, and which can be discovered only by means of thinking. But metaphysical realism cannot at the same time bring itself also to acknowledge the form of being which thinking communicates to it, the concept (the idea), as an equally valid factor along with perception. If one wants to avoid the contradiction of the unperceivable perception, one must acknowledge that, for the relationship between perceptions which is communicated through thinking, there is no other form of existence for us than that of the concept. When one throws out the unjustified part of metaphysical realism, the world presents itself as the sum total of perceptions and their conceptual (ideal) relationships. Then metaphysical realism flows over into a world view which demands, for perception, the principle of perceivability, and for the interrelationships among perceptions, thinkability. This world view can grant no credibility to a third region of the world—besides the perceptual world and the conceptual one—for which both principles, the so-called real principle and the ideal principle, have validity at the same time.

When metaphysical realism asserts that, besides the ideal relationship between the object of perception and its perceiving subject, there must exist in addition a real relationship between the "thing-in-itself" of the perception and the "thing-in-itself" of the perceivable subject (of the so-called individual spirit), then this assertion rests upon the incorrect assumption of an unperceivable real process analogous to the processes of the sense world. When metaphysical realism states further that I come into a consciously ideal relationship with my world of perception, but that I can only come into a dynamic (force) relationship with the real world—then one commits no less the error already criticized. One can speak of a relationship between forces only within the world of perception (in the sphere of the sense of touch), but not outside it.

We shall call the world view characterized above, into which metaphysical realism finally flows when it strips off its contradictory elements, *monism*, because this world view joins one-sided realism with idealism into a higher unity.

For naive realism the real world is a sum of objects of perception; for metaphysical realism, reality is also ascribed to the unperceivable forces, as well as to perceptions; monism replaces the forces with the ideal connections which it gains through thinking. Such connections, however, are the *laws of nature*. A law of nature is indeed nothing more than the conceptual expression for the connection between certain perceptions.

Monism is never put in the position of asking for other principles of explanation for reality besides perception and concept. It knows that within the entire domain of reality there is *no cause* to do so. It sees in the world of perception, as this is directly present to perception, something half real; in uniting the world of perception with the conceptual world it finds the full reality. The metaphysical realist may object to the adherent of monism: It might be the case that for your organization your knowledge is complete in itself, that no part is missing; but you do not know how the world is mirrored in an intelligence organized differently from yours. Monism's answer would be: If there are intelligences other than human ones, and if their perceptions have another form than ours do, then only that has significance for me which reaches me from them through perception and concept. Through my perception, and indeed through my specifically human perception, I am placed as subject over against the object. The connection of things is thereby broken. The subject re-establishes this connection through thinking. It has thereby united itself again with the world whole. Since it is only by our subject that this whole seems to be split at a place between our perception and our concept, so it is that in the reuniting of these two true knowledge is also given. For beings with a different world of perception (for example, with twice our number of sense organs) the connection would appear to be broken at a different place, and its re-establishment would accordingly also have to take a form specific to those beings. Only for naive and metaphysical realism, which both see in the content of the soul only an ideal representation of the world, does the question of a limit to knowledge arise. For them, what is outside the subject is something absolute, something self-contained, and the content of the subject is a picture of it and stands totally outside this absolute. The completeness of one's knowledge depends upon the greater or lesser similarity of one's picture to the absolute object. A being whose number of senses is smaller than man's will perceive less of the world; a being with a larger number, more of it. The former accordingly will have a less complete knowledge than the latter.

Monism sees the matter differently. Through the organization of the perceiving entity, the form is determined as to where the coherency of the world appears torn apart into subject and object. The object is not something absolute, but only something relative with respect to this particular subject. Therefore the bridging over of this antithesis can again only happen in the very specific way precisely characteristic of the human subject. As soon as the "I," which is separated off from the world in perception, joins itself back into coherency with the world again in thinking contemplation, then all further questioning, which was only a consequence of the separation, ceases.

A differently constituted being would have a differently constituted knowledge. Our knowledge suffices to answer the questions posed by our own being.

Metaphysical realism must ask, by what means is what is given as perception given; by what means is the subject affected?

For monism, perception is determined through the subject. But at the same time, the subject has in thinking the means by which to dispel this self-evoked determination again.

Metaphysical realism confronts a further difficulty when it wants to explain the similarity of the world pictures of different human individuals. It must ask itself how it comes about that the picture of the world, which I construct out of my subjectively determined perception and my concepts, is equivalent to the picture which another individual constructs out of the same two subjective factors. How can I, out of my subjective world picture, draw any conclusions at all about that of another person? From the fact that people manage to deal with each other in actual practice, the metaphysical realist believes himself able to infer the similarity of their subjective pictures of the world. From the similarity of these world pictures he then goes on to infer the likeness existing between the individual spirits underlying the single human subjects of perception, or rather between the "I's-in-themselves" underlying the subjects.

This inference is therefore of a kind in which, from a sum of effects, the character of their underlying causes is inferred. We believe, from a sufficiently large number of instances, that we recognize the state of affairs well enough to know how the inferred causes will behave in other instances. We call such an inference an inductive inference. We will see ourselves obliged to modify the results of an inference, if a further observation yields something unexpected, because the character of the result is after all determined only by the individual form of the observations already made. The metaphysical realist claims, however, that this conditional knowledge of the causes is altogether sufficient for practical life.

The inductive inference is the methodological basis of modern metaphysical realism. There was a time when one believed one could unfold something out of concepts which was no longer a concept. One believed that, out of concepts, one could know the metaphysical real beings which metaphysical realism after all needs. This kind of philosophizing has been overcome and is obsolete today. Instead of this, however, one believes that one can infer, from a large enough number of perceptible facts, the character of the thing-in-itself which underlies these facts. Just as formerly from the concept, so today one seeks from our perceptions to be able to unfold the metaphysical. Since one has concepts before oneself in transparent clarity, one believed that one could also derive the metaphysical from them with absolute certainty. Perceptions do not lie before us with the same transparent clarity. Each successive one presents something different again from earlier ones of the same kind. Basically, therefore, what has been inferred from earlier perceptions is somewhat modified by each succeeding one. The form which one wins in this way for the metaphysical must therefore be called only a relatively true one; it is subject to correction through future instances. Eduard von Hartmann's metaphysics has a character determined by this basic, methodological principle; he set as motto on the title page of his first major work: "Speculative results arrived at by the inductive scientific method."

The form which the metaphysical realist today gives to his things-in-themselves is won through inductive inferences. Through his deliberations on the process of knowledge he is convinced of the existence of an objective real coherency of the world alongside the "subjective" coherency knowable through perception and concept. He believes that he can determine, through inductive inferences drawn from his perceptions, how this objective reality is constituted.

Addendum to the Revised Edition of 1918. For the unprejudiced observation of our experience in perception and concept—the description of which has been attempted in the foregoing considerations—certain mental pictures that arise in the field of nature study will again and again be troublesome. One says to oneself, standing in this field, that colors in the light spectrum from red to violet are perceived through the eye. But beyond violet there lie forces within the spectrum's sphere of radiation for which there is no corresponding color perception of the eye, but for which there is definitely a corresponding chemical effect; in the same way, beyond the boundary of red effects, there lie radiations which have only warmth effects. Through consideration of this and similar phenomena, one comes to the view that the scope of the human world of perception is determined by the scope of the human senses, and that man would have a completely different world before him, if he had, in addition to his own senses, still others, or if he had altogether different ones. A person who likes to go off into extravagant fantasies (to which the brilliant discoveries of recent scientific research give a quite enticing stimulus) may very well conclude that into man's field of observation can come only what can act upon those senses which have emerged out of his organization. Man has no right to regard these perceptions, which are limited by his organization, as being in any way conclusive for reality. Every new sense would have to place him before a different picture of reality.—All this is, within appropriate bounds, an altogether justified opinion. But if someone allows this opinion to confuse him in his unprejudiced observation of the relationship between perception and concept which our expositions establish as valid, then he blocks his way to a knowledge of the world and of man that is rooted in reality. The experience of the being of thinking, that is, active working with the world of concepts, is something altogether different from the experience of what is perceivable through the senses. Whatever senses man might ever have in addition to his present ones, not one of them would give him a reality if he did not, in thinking, permeate with concepts the perceptions communicated by it; and every sense, whatever its nature, thus permeated, gives man the possibility of living within reality. Fantasies about the completely different perceptual picture possible with other senses have nothing to do with the question of how the human being stands within the real world. One has to recognize, in fact, that *every* perceptual picture receives its form from the organization of the perceiving entity, but that the perceptual picture, which is permeated by the experience of thinking contemplation, leads the human being into reality. Fantastic depictions of how differently a world would have to appear to other than human senses cannot motivate the human being to seek knowledge about his relationship to the world, but only the insight can do so, that *each* perception gives only a part of the reality contained within it, that it leads, therefore, away from its *own reality*. The other insight then takes its place beside the first, that thinking leads into that part of reality which is present in, but hidden by, the perception itself. It can also be disturbing for the unprejudiced observation of the relationship presented here between perception and concept worked out by thinking, when the necessity arises in the realm of physical experience of speaking, not at all about elements which are directly visible to perception, but rather about invisible magnitudes such as electrical or magnetic lines of forces, and so on. It can *seem* as though the elements of reality about which physics speaks had nothing to do either with what is perceivable, nor with the concept worked out in active thinking. But such an opinion would rest on a self-deception. In the first place it comes down to the fact that *everything* which is worked out by physics, insofar as it does not represent unjustified hypotheses which should be excluded, is won through perception and concept. What seems to be an invisible content is placed, by the physicist's correct instinct for knowledge, totally into the realm in which perceptions lie, and is thought about in concepts with which one is active in this realm. The strengths of electrical and magnetic fields and so on are essentially not found through any process of knowledge other than that which occurs between perception and concept.—Increasing the number, or changing the form, of our human senses would result in a changed perceptual picture, in an enrichment or different form of human experience; but even with respect to *this* experience, a real knowledge would have to be attained through the interaction of concept and perception. Any *deepening* of knowledge depends upon the powers of intuition that live in thinking (see pages 71– 72). This intuition can, within that *experience* which takes shape and is elaborated in thinking, delve down into greater or lesser depths of reality. The broadening of one's perceptual picture can be a stimulus to this delving down and in this way indirectly promote it. But this delving into the depths should *never*, in its attainment of reality, be confused with whether one stands before a broader or more narrow perceptual picture, in which *always* is present only half of reality because of conditions placed on it by the knowing organization. Whoever is not lost in *abstractions* will see how there is relevance for our knowledge of man's nature in the fact that physics must *infer* elements within the realm of perception, to which no sense is directly attuned the way there is to color or tone. The *concrete* nature of man is not only determined by what, through his organization, he places before himself as direct perception, but also through the exclusion of other things from this direct perception. Just as, besides our conscious waking state, the unconscious sleeping state is necessary to life, so, besides the circumference of our sense perception, there is necessary for man's experience of himself, a circumference—much greater in fact—of non-sense-perceptible elements within the realm from which our sense perceptions originate. All this has already been indirectly expressed in the original text of this book. The author adds these amplifications to the content of his book, because it has been his experience that many readers have not read carefully enough.—Attention should also be paid to the fact that the idea of *perception*, as developed in this book, should not be confused with the idea of outer sense perception, which is only a specific instance of the idea of perception. One will see, from the foregoing considerations, but even more from the following ones, that here, everything which approaches man sense-perceptibly *and spiritually*, is regarded as perception, before it is grasped by the actively elaborated concept. In order to have perceptions of a soul or spiritual nature, senses of the kind usually meant are not necessary. One might say that broadening our present use of language in this way is not permissible. But this broadening is *absolutely necessary*, if one does not want to be fettered in certain areas by just such current usage in broadening our knowledge. A person who speaks of perception *only* in the sense of sense perception will also fail to arrive at a concept, adequate for knowledge, concerning *this* sense perception. One *must* oftentimes broaden a concept so that, in a narrower realm, it will gain the meaning appropriate to it. One must also sometimes add something to what was at first meant by a certain concept so that what was thus meant finds its justification or even its correction. Thus, on page 82 of this book, one finds it stated that, "The mental picture is therefore an individualized concept." The objection was made to me that this is an unusual use of language. But this use of language is necessary, if one wants to get behind what a mental picture really is. What would become of our progress in knowledge if the objection were made to everyone who is obliged to set a concept right, that: "That is an unusual use of language?"

THE REALITY OF
SPIRITUAL ACTIVITY (*FREIHEIT*)

VIII
The Factors of Life

Let us recapitulate what we have won in the preceding chapters. The world approaches man as a multiplicity, as a sum of single things. One of these single things, a being among beings, is he himself. We designate this form of the world as simply *given*, and insofar as we do not develop this form through conscious activity, but rather find it before us, we call it *perception*. Within the world of perception we perceive our own self. This self-perception would simply remain there as one perception among the many others, if there did not arise from the midst of this self-perception something which proves itself able to connect all perceptions, and therefore also the sum total of all other perceptions, with that of our self. This something which arises is no longer mere perception; it is also not, like perceptions, simply found before us. It is brought forth through our activity. It seems at first to be bound to what we perceive as our self. In its inner significance, however, it reaches out beyond the self. To the single perceptions it adds ideal characterizations which, however, relate to one another, which are founded in one whole. It characterizes ideally what is won through self-perception in the same way as all other perceptions, and places it as subject or "I" over against the objects. This something is thinking, and the ideal characterizations are concepts and ideas. Thinking manifests itself therefore at first in the perception of the self; it is, however, not merely subjective; for the self first designates itself as subject with the help of thinking. This relationship to itself in thinking is a life characteristic of our personality. Through it we lead a purely ideal existence. We feel ourselves through it to be thinking beings. This life characteristic would remain a purely conceptual (logical) one, if no other characteristics of our self supervened. We would then be beings whose life would be limited to the establishment of purely ideal relationships among our perceptions themselves, and between them and ourselves. If one calls this establishing of such a thought situation "cognizing," and the condition of our self attained through it "knowing," then, if the above supposition applies, we would have to regard ourselves as merely cognizing or knowing beings.

This presupposition, however, does not apply. We do not merely relate our perceptions to ourselves ideally, through the concept, but also through feeling, as we have seen. We are therefore not beings with a merely conceptual content to our lives. The naive realist, in fact, sees in the life of feeling a life of the personality more real than in the purely ideal element of knowing. And from his standpoint he is entirely right when he explains the matter to himself in this way. Feeling, from the subjective side, is at first exactly the same as what perception is from the objective side. According to the basic principle of naive realism that everything is real that can be perceived: feeling is therefore the guarantee of the reality of one's own personality. The monism presented here must, however, confer upon feeling the same complement that it considers necessary for any perception, if perception is to represent full reality. For this monism, feeling is something real but incomplete which, in the first form in which it is given to us, does not yet contain its second factor: the concept or idea. Therefore feeling also arises everywhere in life, as perceiving does, *before* the activity of knowing. We feel ourselves at first as existing entities; and only in the course of gradual development do we struggle through to the point where, within our own dimly felt existence, the concept of our self arises for us. What *for us* only emerges later is, however, inseparably bound up with our feeling from the beginning. Because of this fact the naive person falls into the belief that in feeling, existence presents itself to him directly; in knowing, only indirectly. The cultivation of his feeling life will therefore seem to him more important than anything else. He will believe that he has grasped the connection of things only when he has taken it up into his feeling. He seeks to make not knowing, but rather feeling, into his means of knowledge. Since feeling is something altogether individual, something equivalent to perception, the philosopher of feeling makes a principle that has significance only within his personality into a world principle. He seeks to permeate the whole world with his own self. What the monism meant here strives to grasp with the concept, this the philosopher of feeling seeks to attain with his feeling, and sees his way of being with objects as the more direct one.

The tendency characterized here as the philosophy of feeling is often termed *mysticism*. The error of a mystical way of viewing things based on feeling alone consists in the fact that it wants to *experience* what it should know, that it wants to transform something individual, feeling, into something universal.

Feeling is a purely individual act, the relating of the outer world to our subject, insofar as this relationship finds its expression in a merely subjective experiencing.

There is still another manifestation of the human personality. The "I" lives along, through its thinking, with the general life of the world; through thinking, in a purely ideal (conceptual) way, it relates its perceptions to itself, and itself to its perceptions. In feeling, the "I" experiences a relationship of the object to itself as subject; in *willing*, the opposite is the case. In willing we likewise have a perception before us, namely that of the individual relationship of our self to what is objective. Whatever in my willing is not a purely ideal factor is just as much a mere object of perception as is the case with any thing in the outer world.

In spite of this, naive realism will believe that here again it has before itself a far more real existence than can be attained through thinking. It will see in willing an element within which it becomes *directly* conscious of a happening, of bringing something about, in contrast to thinking, which first grasps the happening in concepts. What the "I" accomplishes through this willing represents, for this way of viewing things, a process which is directly experienced. In willing, the adherent of this philosophy believes that he has really grasped world happening by one tip. While he can follow other happenings only through perception from outside, he believes that in his willing he experiences a real happening quite directly. The form of existence in which his will appears to him within the self becomes for him a real principle of reality. His own willing appears to him as a specific case of universal world happening; and this latter appears, therefore, as universal willing. Will becomes the world principle just as, in the mysticism of feeling, feeling becomes the knowledge principle. This way of viewing things is *philosophy of will* (thelism). Something which can only be experienced individually is made by this philosophy into the factor constitutive of the world.

Just as little as mysticism of feeling can be called science, can philosophy of will be so called. For both assert that they cannot make do with a conceptual penetration of the world. Both demand, besides the ideal principle of existence, a real principle as well. And this with a certain justification. But since we have, for this so-called real principle, only our perception as a means of grasping it, so this assertion of the mysticism of feeling and of the philosophy of will is identical with the view that we have two sources of knowledge: that of thinking and that of perceiving; and this latter presents itself in feeling and will as individual experience. Since what flows from the one source, the experiences, cannot be taken up by these world views directly into what flows from the other source, that of thinking, these two ways of knowledge, perceiving and thinking, continue to exist side by side without any higher mediation. Besides the ideal principle attainable through knowing, there is supposedly still a real principle of the world in addition, which is experienceable but not to be grasped in thinking. In other words: mysticism of feeling and philosophy of will are naive realism, because they subscribe to the proposition that what is directly perceived is real. Only, with respect to original naive realism, they commit in addition the inconsistency of making one particular form of perception (feeling, or willing as the case may be) into the only means of knowing existence, which they can do, after all, only if they subscribe in general to the basic proposition that what is perceived is real. Therefore they would also have to ascribe to outer perception an equal cognitive value.

Philosophy of will becomes metaphysical realism when it also transfers will into *those* spheres of existence in which—unlike in one's own subject—a direct experience of will is not possible. It assumes hypothetically a principle outside the subject, for which subjective experience is the sole criterion of reality. As metaphysical realism, the philosophy of will falls under the critique, presented in the preceding chapter, which overcomes and acknowledges the contradictory factor in any kind of metaphysical realism, which is that will is a universal world happening only insofar as it relates itself ideally to the rest of the world.

Addendum to the Revised Edition of 1918. The difficulty in grasping thinking in its essential being by observing it lies in the fact that this essential being has all too easily slipped away already from the observing soul when the soul wants to bring this being into its line of vision. There then remains for the soul only the dead abstractness, the corpse of living thinking. If one looks only upon this abstractness, one can easily find oneself impelled, in the face of it, to enter into the "life-filled" element of the mysticism of feeling or else of metaphysics of the will. One can find it strange that someone should want to grasp, in "mere thought," the essential being of reality. But whoever brings himself to the point of truly having *life in his thinking* will attain the insight that neither weaving in mere feelings nor looking upon the will element can even be compared to the inner wealth and to the peaceful, self-sustaining, yet inwardly moving *experience* within this life of thinking, let alone that these two could be ranked above it. It is precisely due to this wealth, to this inner fullness of experience, that thinking's counterpart in our usual state of soul appears dead, abstract. No other human soul activity is so easy to misapprehend as thinking. Willing, feeling: they warm the human soul, even in one's reliving of the original experiences. Thinking all too easily leaves one cold in this reliving; it seems to dry out one's soul life. But this is only the strongly manifesting shadow of thinking's reality—a reality which is woven through with light, and which delves down warmly into the phenomena of the world. This delving down occurs through a power that flows within the thinking activity itself, which is the power of love in spiritual form. One may not raise the objection that whoever, in this way, sees love within active thinking is transferring a feeling, love, into it. For this objection is in truth a confirmation of what is being maintained here. Whoever turns, namely, *to* thinking in its *essential being*, will find in it both feeling and will, and these also in the depths of their reality; whoever turns away from thinking and toward "mere" feeling and willing only, will lose their true reality. Whoever wants to *experience intuitively* within thinking is also doing justice to experience of a feeling and will nature; the mysticism of feeling and the metaphysics of will, however, cannot do justice to the intuitive thinking penetration of existence. These last can all too easily come to the opinion that *they* stand within what is real, but that the intuitively thinking person, unfeeling and estranged from reality, forms with his "abstract thoughts" a shadowy, cold world picture.

IX
The Idea of Spiritual Activity (*Freiheit*)

The concept of a tree, for my activity of knowing, is conditional upon my perception of the tree. With respect to a particular perception I can lift only one particular concept out of my general system of concepts. The connection between concept and perception is indirectly and objectively determined by thinking in accordance with the perception. The connection of the perception with its concept is known after the act of perception; their belonging together, however, is determined within the thing itself.

The process presents itself differently when knowledge, when the relationship of man to the world which arises in knowledge, is regarded. In the preceding considerations the attempt was made to show that a clarifying of this relationship is possible when an unprejudiced observation is directed upon it. A right understanding of such observation comes to the insight that thinking, as a self-contained entity, can be looked upon directly. Whoever finds it necessary for the explanation of thinking as such to draw upon something else—physical brain processes, for example, or unconscious spiritual processes lying behind our perceived conscious thinking—fails to recognize what the unprejudiced observation of thinking gives him. Whoever observes thinking lives during his observation directly within a spiritual, self-sustaining weaving of being. Yes, one can say that whoever wants to grasp the being of the spiritual in the form in which it *first* presents itself to man, can do this within thinking which is founded upon itself.

When thinking itself is regarded, there merge into one what otherwise *must* always appear separately: concept and perception. Whoever does not recognize this will be able to see, in the concepts he works out with respect to his perceptions, only shadowy copies of these perceptions, and his perceptions will represent for him true reality. He will also build up for himself a metaphysical world modeled upon the perceived world; he will call this world the world of atoms, the world of will, unconscious spirit world, and so on, according to his particular way of picturing things. And it will escape him that in all this he has only hypothetically built himself a metaphysical world modeled upon *his* world of perception. Whoever does recognize, however, what lies before him with respect to thinking, will know that in the perception only a part of reality is present before him, and that the other part belonging to the perception, which alone first allows it to appear as full reality, will be *experienced* in his thinking permeation of the perception. He will not see, in what arises as thinking in his consciousness, a shadowy copy of a reality, but rather self-sustaining, spiritual, essential being. And about this essential being he can say that it is present for him in his consciousness through *intuition. Intuition* is the conscious experience, occurring within the purely spiritual, of a purely spiritual content. Only through an intuition can the being of thinking be grasped.

Only when one has struggled through to the recognition—won through unprejudiced observation—of this truth about the intuitive nature of thinking, will the way be successfully cleared for a view of the human physical and soul organization. One recognizes that this organization can bring about *nothing* with respect to the *essential being* of thinking. Completely obvious facts *seem*, at first, to contradict this. Human thinking appears for ordinary experience only in connection with and through this organization. This appearance makes itself felt so strongly that it can only be seen in its true significance by someone who has recognized how nothing plays into the essential being of thinking from this organization. But then such a person can also not fail to see how particular the nature of the relation of the human organization to thinking is. This organization brings about nothing with respect to the essential being of thinking, but rather draws back when the activity of thinking appears; it ceases its own activity; it frees up a place; and upon the place now freed, thinking appears. The essential being which works within thinking has a double task: first, it represses the human organization's own activity, and secondly, it sets itself in the place of this activity. For the repressing of the bodily organization is also the result of thinking activity. And indeed, of that part of thinking activity which prepares for the *appearance* of thinking. One sees from this in what sense thinking finds its counterpart in the bodily organization. And when one sees this, one will no longer be able to misapprehend the significance of this counterpart for thinking itself. If someone walks over soft ground, his feet leave prints in the ground. One would not be tempted to say that the forms of the footprints were pushed in by forces of the earth working up from beneath. One would ascribe to *these* forces no part in the coming about of the forms of the prints. Just as little would someone who observes the being of thinking without prejudice ascribe to the imprints in the bodily organization a part in the coming about of the being of thinking; these imprints arise through the fact that thinking prepares its appearance through the body.*

However, a significant question arises here. If the human organization has no part in the *essential being* of thinking, what significance does this organization have within the total being of man? Now, what occurs within this organization through thinking has, indeed, nothing to do with the being of thinking; but it has very much to do with the arising of "I"-consciousness out of this thinking. Within thinking's one being there lies, indeed, the real "I," but not "I"-consciousness. The person who actually observes thinking without prejudice recognizes this. The "I" is to be found within thinking; "I-consciousness" arises through the fact that in ordinary consciousness the traces of thinking activity imprint themselves in the sense described above. (Through the bodily

---

*In other writings that have followed this book the author has shown how the above view is confirmed in psychology, physiology, etc. This account intends only to characterize what is yielded by unprejudiced observation of thinking.

organization, therefore, "I"-consciousness arises. One should not confuse this, however, with any kind of assertion that "I"-consciousness, once it has arisen, remains dependent upon the bodily organization. Once arisen, it is taken up into thinking and shares from then on in thinking's spiritual nature.)

"I-consciousness" is built upon the human organization. From this organization flow the actions of the will. According to the direction of what has been presented thus far, an insight into the relationship between thinking, conscious "I," and acts of will, is only to be attained if one first observes how the act of will goes forth from the human organization.*

For the individual act of will there come into consideration: motive and mainspring of action. The motive is a conceptual or mentally-pictured factor; the mainspring of action is the directly conditioning factor of willing in the human organization. The conceptual factor or the motive is the momentary determining factor of willing; the mainspring of action is the lasting determining factor of the individual person. Motive for willing can be a pure concept or a concept with a definite relation to perception, that is, a mental picture. General and individual concepts (mental pictures) become motives for willing through the fact that they affect the human individual and determine his action in a certain direction. One and the same concept, or one and the same mental picture, as the case may be, affects different individuals differently, however. They

---

*Page 130 to the above sentence is an addition, or, as the case may be, reworking for the revised edition of 1918.

move different people to different actions. Willing is therefore not merely a result of the concept or mental picture, but rather of the individual make-up of the person as well. Let us call this individual make-up—we can follow Eduard von Hartmann in this respect—the characterological disposition. The way in which concept and mental picture affect the characterological disposition of a person gives a definite moral or ethical stamp to his life.

The characterological disposition is formed through the more or less lasting life-content of our subject, i.e., through our content of mental pictures and feelings. Whether a mental picture, arising in me at the moment, stimulates me to will something or not, depends upon how it relates to the content of the rest of my mental pictures and also to my peculiarities of feeling. My content of mental pictures, however, is again determined by the sum total of those concepts which in the course of my individual life have come into contact with perceptions, that means, have become mental pictures. This again depends upon my greater or lesser capacity for intuition and upon the scope of my observations, that is, upon the subjective and objective factors of my experiences, upon inner determinants and location in life. My characterological disposition is most especially determined by my life of feeling. Whether I feel pleasure or pain with respect to a definite mental picture or concept, upon this will depend whether I want to make it a motive for my action or not.—These are the elements which come into consideration with respect to an act of will. The immediately present mental picture or concept which becomes my motive determines the goal, the purpose of my willing; my characterological disposition moves me to direct my activity toward this goal. The mental picture of taking a walk in the next half hour determines the goal of my action. But this mental picture will only then be raised into a motive for willing when it hits upon an appropriate characterological disposition, that is, when, through my life up till now, mental pictures have formed in me as to the purposes for taking a walk, as to the value of healthiness, and furthermore, when in me the feeling of pleasure unites with the mental picture of taking a walk.

We have therefore to distinguish: 1. The possible subjective dispositions appropriate to making particular mental pictures and concepts into motives; and 2. the possible mental pictures and concepts capable of influencing my characterological disposition in such a way that willing results. The former represent the *mainsprings*, the latter the *goals* of morality.

The mainsprings of morality we can find by examining what are the elements out of which our individual life is composed.

The first level of our individual life is *perceiving*, more particularly, perceiving with the senses. We stand here in that region of our individual life where perceiving passes over directly into willing, without any feeling or concept coming in between. The human mainspring of action which comes into consideration here is simply called *drive*. The satisfaction of our lower, purely animal needs (hunger, sexual intercourse, etc.) comes about in this way. The characteristic feature of the life of drives consists in the immediacy with which the individual perception activates the will. This way of determining the will, which originally is peculiar only to the lower life of the senses, can also be extended to the perceptions of the higher senses. With the perception of some sort of happening in the outer world, without further reflection, and without any particular feeling in us connecting itself to the perception, we let there follow an action, as this happens especially in conventional social life. One calls the mainspring for this action *tact* or *social propriety*. The more often there occurs such an immediate causing of an action through a perception, the more will the person concerned show himself inclined to act purely under the influence of tact, that is: *tact* becomes his characterological disposition.

The second sphere of human life is *feeling.* Onto my perceptions of the outer world, specific feelings connect themselves. These feelings can become mainsprings of action. If I see a starving person, my pity for him can represent the mainspring of my action. Such feelings are for example: the feeling of shame, pride, sense of honor, modesty, remorse, pity, the feelings of vengefulness and gratitude, reverence, faithfulness, the feelings of love and duty.*

The third level of life, finally, is *thinking and mental picturing*. Through mere reflection a mental picture or a concept can become the motive for an action. Mental pictures become motives through the fact that in the course of life we continuously connect certain goals of our will with perceptions which recur again and again in more or

---

*One can find a complete compilation of the principles of morality (from the standpoint of metaphysical realism) in Eduard von Hartmann's *Phenomenology of Moral Consciousness* (*Phaenomenologie des sittlichen Bewusstseins*).

less modified form. This accounts for the fact that with people who are not entirely without experience, there always arise in their consciousness, along with particular perceptions, also mental pictures of actions which they have carried out in a similar case or have seen carried out. These mental pictures hover before them as determining models in all future decisions; they become part of their characterological disposition. We may call the mainsprings of will just described *practical experience*. Practical experience passes over gradually into purely tactful action. When certain typical pictures of actions have united themselves in our consciousness so firmly with mental pictures of certain situations in life that in a given case we skip all reflection based on experience and go directly from the perception into willing, then this is the case.

The highest level of individual life is conceptual thinking without regard to a specific content of perception. We determine the content of a concept through pure intuition out of the ideal sphere. Such a concept then contains, to begin with, no relation to specific perceptions. When, under the influence of a concept which points to a perception—that is, under the influence of a mental picture—we enter into willing, then it is this perception that determines us in a roundabout way through conceptual thinking. When we act under the influence of intuitions, then the mainspring of our action is *pure thinking*. Since one is used, in philosophy, to calling the ability of pure thinking "reason," so one is also fully justified in calling the mainsprings of morality on the level just characterized, *practical reason*. The clearest account of these mainsprings of will has been given by Kreyenbühl ("Philosophical

Monthly,''★ Vol. XVIII, No. 3). I consider his article on this subject to be one of the most significant creations of modern philosophy, more particularly of ethics. Kreyen-bühl describes the mainsprings of action we are discussing as *practical a priori*, that means an impulse to action flowing directly out of my intuition.

It is clear that such an impulse can, in the strict sense of the word, no longer be considered as belonging to the sphere of my characterological disposition. For, what works here as mainspring is no longer something individual in me, but rather the ideal and therefore universal content of my intuition. As soon as I recognize the validity of this content as a foundation and starting point for an action, I enter into willing, regardless of whether the concept was already there within me beforehand in time, or only entered my consciousness immediately before my action; that is, regardless of whether the concept was already present in me as predisposition or not.

It then comes to a real act of will only when a momentary impulse of action, in the form of a concept or mental picture, works upon the characterological disposition. Such an impulse then becomes the motive of willing.

The motives of morality are mental pictures and concepts. There are philosophers of ethics who also see in feeling a motive of morality; they maintain, for example, that the goal of moral action is the promotion of the greatest possible amount of pleasure within the individual acting. The pleasure itself, however, cannot become a motive, but only a *mentally pictured pleasure*. The *mental*

★*Philosophische Monatshefte.*

picture of a future feeling, but not the feeling itself, however, can work upon my characterological disposition. For in the moment of the action the feeling itself is not yet there: it is meant, in fact, first to be effected through the action.

The *mental picture* of one's own or of someone else's good, however, is rightly regarded as a motive of willing. The principle of causing through one's action the greatest amount of pleasure to oneself, that is, of attaining individual happiness, is called *egoism*. One seeks to attain this individual happiness either through the fact that one thinks ruthlessly of one's own good only, and strives for this at the cost of the happiness of other individuals (pure egoism), or through the fact that one promotes the good of others because one anticipates indirectly a favorable influence upon one's own person from the happiness of these other individualities, or because one fears, through the harming of other individuals, also the endangering of one's own interests (morality of prudence). The particular content of the principles of egoistic morality will depend upon what mental picture a person makes for himself of his own or of another's happiness. According to what a person regards as a good thing in life (luxury, hope of happiness, deliverance from various misfortunes, etc.), he will determine the content of his egoistical striving.

One can then regard the purely conceptual content of an action as a further motive. This content does not, like the mental picture of one's own pleasure, relate itself to the single action only, but rather to the founding of its action out of a system of moral principles. These moral principles, in the form of abstract concepts, can regulate one's moral life, without one bothering about the origin of the concepts. We then simply feel our submission to the moral concept, which hovers over our action like a commandment, as moral necessity. We leave the founding of this necessity to the one who demands the moral submission, that is, to the moral authority whom we acknowledge (head of the family, state, social custom, authority of the church, divine revelation). One instance of these principles of morality is that in which the commandment does not make itself known to us through an outer authority, but rather through our own inner life (moral autonomy). We then perceive within our own inner life the voice to which we must submit. The expression of this voice is *conscience.*

It signifies moral progress when a person no longer simply takes the commandment of an outer or inner authority as the motive of his action, but rather when his striving is for insight into the reason why one or another maxim of action should work in him as motive. This progress is one from authoritative morality to action out of moral insight. At this level of morality the person will seek out the needs of moral life and will allow himself to be determined in his actions by his knowledge of them. Such needs are: 1. the greatest possible good of all mankind, purely for the sake of this good; 2. cultural progress or the moral *development* of mankind to ever greater perfection; 3. the realization of individual goals of morality grasped purely intuitively. The *greatest possible good of all mankind* will naturally be comprehended by different people in different ways. The above maxim does not refer to a particular mental picture of this good, but rather to the fact that each person who acknowledges this principle strives to do what, in his view, best promotes the good of all mankind.

Cultural progress is seen, by the person in whom a feeling of pleasure is united with the good things of culture, to be a special case of the foregoing moral principle. He will only have to take into the bargain the downfall and destruction of many things which also contribute to the good of mankind. It is, however, also possible that a person sees in cultural progress, aside from any feeling of pleasure connected with it, a moral necessity. Then this progress is for him a moral principle of its own beside the foregoing one.

Both the maxim of the good of all and that of cultural progress are based upon the mental picture, that is, upon the relation one gives the content of moral ideas to specific experiences (perceptions). The highest conceivable principle of morality is, however, the one which from the beginning contains no such relation but rather springs from the source of pure intuition and only afterward seeks a relation to perception (to life). The determining of what is to be willed goes forth here from a different quarter than in the foregoing cases. The person who holds to the moral principle of the good of all, will, in all his actions, first ask what his ideals contribute to this good of all. The person who subscribes to the moral principle of cultural progress will do the same thing here. There is, however, a higher principle which, in each individual case, does not start from one particular single goal of morality, but which rather attaches to all maxims of morality a certain value, and, in any given case always asks whether one or another moral principle is more important. It can happen that someone will, under certain circumstances, regard the promotion of cultural progress as the right principle and make it the motive of his action, under others, the promotion of the good of all, in a third case, the promotion of his own good. But only when all other determining factors take second place does conceptual intuition itself then come first and foremost into consideration. Other motives thereby step back from their leading position, and only the ideal content of the action works as its motive.

Of the levels of the characterological disposition, we have designated that one as the highest which works as *pure thinking*, as *practical reason*. Of motives, we have just now designated as the highest *conceptual intuition*. Upon closer reflection, it immediately turns out to be the case that at this level of morality, mainspring of action and motive coincide, that is, neither a predetermined characterological disposition nor an outer moral principle accepted as norm affects our action. The action is therefore not stereotyped, carried out according to some rule or other, and also not of the kind which a person performs automatically in response to an outer impetus, but rather one determined purely and simply by its ideal content.

A prerequisite for such an action is the capacity for moral intuitions. Whoever lacks the capacity to experience the particular maxim of morality for each individual case, will also never achieve truly individual willing.

The exact antithesis of this principle of morality is the Kantian one: Act in such a way that the basic tenets of your action can be valid for all men. This principle is the death of all individual impulse to action. Not how *all* men would act can be decisive for me, but rather what for me is to be done in the individual case.

A superficial judgment could perhaps object to this: How can your actions at the same time be shaped individually toward a particular case and a particular situation, and still be determined in a purely ideal way out of intuition? This objection rests on a confusion of moral motive with the perceptible content of an action. The latter *can* be a motive, and is, for example, in cultural progress, in action out of egoism, etc.; in action based upon purely moral intuition, it is *not* a motive. My "I" of course directs its gaze upon this content of perception; the "I" does not allow itself to be *determined* by it. This content is used only in order to form for oneself a *cognitive concept*; the *moral concept* belonging to it, this the "I" does not take from the object. The cognitive concept of a particular situation which I am confronting is only then at the same time a moral concept if I am standing upon the standpoint of a particular moral principle. If I would like to stand upon the ground of the principle of cultural development alone, then I would go around in the world with fixed marching orders. From every happening that I perceive and that can concern me, there springs at the same time a moral duty; namely, to do my bit so that the particular happening is placed in the service of cultural development. In addition to the concept, which reveals to me the connections of natural law of a happening or thing, there is also hung upon the happening or thing a moral etiquette, which contains for me, the moral being, an ethical directive as to how I am to conduct myself. This moral etiquette is justified in its sphere; it coincides, however, from a higher standpoint, with the idea which occurs to me when confronted by a concrete case.

People are different in their capacity for intuition. In one the ideas bubble up; another acquires them for himself laboriously. The situations in which people live and which provide the stage for their actions are no less different. How a person acts will therefore depend on the way his capacity for intuition works in a given situation. What determines the sum total of the ideas active within us, the real content of our intuitions, is that which, in spite of the universality of the world of ideas, is individually constituted in every person. Insofar as this intuitive content passes over into action, it is the moral content of the individual. Allowing this content to live itself out is the highest moral mainspring of action, and at the same time the highest motive, of the person who sees that all other moral principles, in the last analysis, unite in this content. One can call this standpoint *ethical individualism.*

The decisive factor for an intuitively determined action in a concrete case is the finding of the appropriate, completely individual intuition. On this level of morality it can be a question of general moral concepts (norms, laws) only insofar as these result from the generalizing of individual impulses. General norms always presuppose concrete facts from which they can be derived. Through human action, however, facts are first *created.*

When we seek out the lawful (the conceptual in the actions of individuals, peoples, and epochs), we do obtain an ethics, not as a science of moral norms, however, but rather as a natural history of morality. Only the laws won in this way relate to human action the way natural laws relate to a particular phenomenon. These laws, however, are not at all identical with the impulses upon which we base our actions. If someone wants to grasp how a person's action springs from his *moral* willing, then he must look first of all at the relationship of this willing to the action. He must first of all take a good look at actions for which this relationship is the determining factor. When I or someone else thinks back over such an action later, one can discover what moral maxims come into consideration for that action. While I am acting, the moral maxim is moving me, insofar as it can live in me intuitively; it is bound up with my *love* for the object which I want to realize through my action. I ask no person nor any rule: Ought I to carry out this action?—rather, I carry it out as soon as I have grasped the idea of it. Only through this is it *my* action. The action of someone who acts only because he acknowledges certain moral norms is the result of the principles which stand in his moral codex. He is merely the executor. He is a higher kind of automaton. Throw a stimulus to action into his consciousness, and immediately the cogwheels of his moral principles are set into motion and turn in a lawful manner to execute a Christian, humane, to him selfless action; or one of cultural-historical progress. Only when I follow my love for the object is it I myself who acts. I act on this level of morality, not because I acknowledge a master over me, nor outer authority, nor a so-called inner voice. I acknowledge no outer principle for my action, because I have found within myself the basis for my actions: love for the action. I do not test intellectually, whether my action is good or evil; I carry it out because I *love* it. It will be "good" when my intuition, imbued with love, stands in the right way within the intuitively experienceable world configuration; "evil" when that is not the case. I also do not ask myself how another person would act in my position—but rather I act as I, this specific individuality, see myself moved to will. It is not what is generally done, the general custom, a general human maxim, a social norm, which leads me directly, but rather my love for the deed. I feel no compulsion, neither the compulsion of nature which leads me in the case of my drives, nor the compulsion of moral commandments, but rather I simply want to carry out what lives within me.

The defenders of general moral norms could respond to this: If every person strove to live out fully what is in him, and to do whatever he pleases, then there is no difference between good conduct and criminal behavior; any knavery that lives in me has the same right to live itself out as the intention of serving what is universally best. The fact that I have scrutinized an action from the ideal point of view cannot be the decisive factor for me as a moral person, but rather my testing as to whether it is good or *evil*. Only when the former is the case will I carry out the action.

My answer to this objection, which is obvious, but which nevertheless springs only from a faulty understanding of what is meant here, is this: Whoever wants to know the nature of human willing must distinguish between the path which brings this willing up to a certain level of development, and the particular nature which this willing acquires when it nears this goal. On the way to this goal, norms play their justified role. The goal consists in the realization of moral goals which are grasped purely by intuition. A person attains such goals to the extent that he possesses the ability to lift himself at all to the intuitive idea-content of the world. In individual cases of willing, other mainsprings of action or other motives will usually be mixed in with such goals. But what is intuitive can still be a determining or codetermining factor in human willing. What one *ought* to do, this one does; one provides the stage upon which "ought to" becomes doing; one's own action is what one allows to spring from one-. self. There the impulse can only be a completely individual one. And, in truth, only an act of will which springs from an intuition can be an individual one. That the act of the criminal, that something evil, might be called the expressing of one's individuality, in the same sense as the embodiment of pure intuition, is possible only if blind drives are reckoned as part of the human individuality. But the blind drive which moves one to commit a crime does not stem from anything intuitive, and does not belong to what is individual in man, but rather to what is the most common in him, to that which prevails in all individuals to the same extent, and out of which a person extricates himself through what is individual in him. What is individual in me is not my organism with its drives and feelings, but rather the unified world of ideas which lights up within this organism. My drives, instincts, and passions establish nothing more about me than that I belong to the general species *man*; the fact that something ideal expresses itself in a particular way within these drives, passions, and feelings, establishes my individuality. Through my instincts, drives, I am a person of whom there are twelve to the dozen; through the particular form of the idea by which I designate myself as "I" within this dozen, I am an individual. Going by the difference of my animal nature, only a being other than myself could distinguish me from others; through my thinking, that means, through the active grasping of what expresses itself as something ideal within my organism, I myself distinguish myself from others. Therefore one cannot say at all of the action of the criminal that it goes forth from the idea. That is, in fact, exactly what is characteristic of criminal actions, that they issue from the non-ideal elements of the human being.

An action is felt to be free to the extent that its reason stems from the ideal part of my individual being; every other part of an action, regardless of whether this part is performed under the compulsion of nature or the constraint of a moral norm, is felt to be *unfree*.

A person is free only insofar as he is in a position at every moment of his life to follow himself. A moral act is *my* act only when it can be called free in this sense. Here, our considerations have first of all to do with the prerequisites under which a willed action is felt to be free; how this idea of inner freedom, grasped in a purely ethical way, realizes itself within the being of man, will appear in what follows.

An action out of inner freedom does not by any means exclude the laws of morality, but rather includes them; it only proves to be on a higher level when compared to an action which is only dictated by these laws. Why then should my action serve the universal good any less when I have done it out of love, than when I have performed it *only* because I feel it is my duty to serve the universal good? The bare concept of duty excludes *inner freedom*, because it does not want to acknowledge what is individual, but rather demands submission of the latter to a general norm. Inner freedom of action is conceivable only from the standpoint of ethical individualism.

But how is it possible for people to live together, if everyone is striving only to bring his own individuality into effect? This objection is indicative of a wrongly understood moralism. This moralism believes that a community of people is possible only when they are all united through a communally established moral order. This moralism does not, in fact, understand the unity of the world of ideas. It does not comprehend that the world of ideas active within me is no other than that within my fellowman. This oneness is, to be sure, only the result of experience of the world. But this oneness *must* be such a result. For were this oneness to be known through anything other than through observation, then, in the realm of this oneness, individual experience would not be in force, but rather the general norm. Individuality is possible only when each individual being knows of the other only through individual observation. The difference between me and my fellowman does not lie at all in our living in two completely different spiritual worlds, but rather in the fact that he receives other intuitions than I do out of the world of ideas common to us both. He wants to live out *his* intuitions, I *mine*. If we both really draw from the idea, and follow no outer (physical or spiritual) impulses, then we can only meet each other in the same striving, in the same intentions. A moral misunderstanding, a clash with each other, for morally *free* people is out of the question. Only the morally unfree person, who follows nature's drives or a commandment he takes as duty, thrusts aside his fellowmen if they do not follow the same instinct and the same commandment as he himself. *To live* in the love for one's actions, and *to let live* in understanding for the other's willing, is the basic maxim of *free human beings*. They know no other *"ought"* than that with which their willing brings itself into intuitive harmony; what they shall *will* in a certain case, this their capacity for ideas will tell them.

If the primal basis for sociability did not lie within man's nature, one would not be able to instill it into human nature through any outer laws! Only because human individuals *are* of one spirit are they also able to live and act side by side. The free person lives in the confidence that any other free person belongs with him to one spiritual world and will concur with him in his intentions. The free person demands no agreement from his fellowmen, but he expects agreement, because it lies within man's nature. This does not refer to the necessities which exist for certain external regulations, but rather to the *attitude*, to the *soul disposition*, through which the human being, in his experience of himself among his fellowmen whom he values, most does justice to human worth and dignity.

There are many who will say to this: the concept of the *free* person, which you are sketching here, is a chimera, is nowhere realized. We, however, have to do with real people, and with them one can hope for morality only when they obey a moral commandment, when they conceive of their moral mission as a duty and do not freely follow their inclinations and love.—I do not doubt this at all. Only a blind person could. But then away with all this hypocrisy about morality, if this is supposed to be the *final* word. Just say then that human nature must be *compelled* to its actions as long as it is not *free*. Whether one controls this non-freedom through physical means or through moral laws, whether a person is unfree because he follows his unlimited sexual drive, or because he is bound in the fetters of conventional morality, is, from a certain standpoint, a matter of complete indifference. But one should not claim that such a person can rightly call an action *his own*, since he is after all driven to it by a force other than himself. But out of the midst of such enforced order,. those people lift themselves, the *free spirits*, who find *themselves*, within the welter of custom, law's coercion, religious practice, and so on. They are *free* insofar as they follow only themselves, *unfree*, insofar as they surrender themselves. Who of us can say that he is really free in all his actions? But in each one of us dwells a deeper being, in whom the free person expresses himself.

Our life is constituted of actions of freedom and of non-freedom. We cannot, however, think the concept of man to its conclusion, without our coming upon the *free spirit* as the purest expression of man's nature. Indeed, we are truly human only insofar as we are free.

Many will say that this is an ideal. Doubtless; but it is an ideal that, within our being, does work its way to the surface as a real element. It is no thought-up or dreamed-up ideal, but rather one that has life and that clearly makes

itself known even in the most imperfect form of its existence. Were man merely a being of nature, then his seeking of ideals, that is, his seeking of ideas which at the moment are inoperative, but whose realization is called for,
would be nonsensical. It is by the thing in the outer world
that the idea is determined through perception; we have
done our part when we have recognized the connection
between the idea and the perception. With man this is
not so. The sum total of his existence is not determined
without man himself; his true concept as *moral* human
being (free spirit) is not already objectively united
beforehand with the perceptual picture "human being,"
and merely needing afterward to be ascertained through
knowledge. The human being must, through his own activity, unite his concept with his perception of the human
being. Here concept and perception coincide only if the
human being himself brings them into coincidence. He
can do this, however, only if he has found the concept of
the free spirit, that is, his own concept. Within the world
of objects, because of our organization, a boundary line is
drawn for us between perception and concept; our activity
of knowing overcomes this boundary. Within our subjective nature this boundary is no less present; the human
being overcomes it in the course of his development by
giving shape to his concept in his outer manifestation.
Thus, both the intellectual and the moral life of the
human being lead us to his twofold nature: perceiving
(direct experience) and thinking. His intellectual life
overcomes his twofold nature through knowledge; his
moral life does so by actually realizing the free spirit. Every
being has its inborn concept (the law of its existence and

working); but in outer things the concept is indivisibly united with the perception, and only within our spiritual organism is it separated from this perception. For the human being himself, concept and perception are at first *actually* separated, to be just as *actually* united by him. Someone could object that to our perception of the human being there corresponds at every moment of his life a particular concept, just as with everything else. I can form for myself the concept of an average person and can have such a person also given to me as perception; if I bring to this concept that of the free spirit as well, then I have two concepts for the same object.

That is one-sided thinking. As object of perception, I am subject to continual change. As a child I was different; different again as a young person and as an adult. At every moment, in fact, my perceptible picture is different than in the preceding ones. These changes can occur in the sense that in them the same one (average person) is always expressing himself, or that they represent the manifestation of the free spirit. It is to these changes that my actions, as object of perception, are subject.

There is given to the human being as object of perception the possibility of transforming himself just as, within the seed, there lies the possibility of becoming a whole plant. The plant will transform itself because of the objective lawfulness lying within it; the human being remains in his unfinished state if he does not take up the stuff of transformation within himself and transform himself through his own power. Nature makes out of man merely a being of nature; society, a lawfully acting one; a *free* being, only he *himself* can make out of himself. Nature releases man from its fetters at a certain stage of his development; society leads this development to a certain point; the finishing touches only man can give to himself.

The standpoint of free morality does not maintain, therefore, that the free spirit is the only form in which a human being can exist. It sees in free spirituality only the human being's last stage of development. This does not deny the fact that actions according to norms do have their justification as one level of development. But these actions cannot be regarded as the absolute standpoint of morality. The free spirit, however, overcomes norms in the sense that he does not only feel commandments as motives, but rather directs his actions according to his impulses (intuitions).

When Kant says of duty: "Duty! You great and sublime name! You who include within yourself nothing beloved which bears an ingratiating character, but demand submission," you who "set up a law . . ., before which all inclinations grow silent, even though they secretly work against it,"* then, out of the consciousness of the free spirit, the human being replies, "Freedom! You friendly human name! You who include within yourself everything morally beloved, which my humanity values most, and who makes me the servant of no one; you who do not merely set up a law, but who rather awaits what my moral love itself will acknowledge as law, because this love feels itself to be unfree when faced with any law only forced upon it."

That is the contrast between a merely law-abiding and a free morality.

*Critique of Practical Reason (Kritik der praktischen Vernunft).

The philistine, who sees in something outwardly established morality incarnate will perhaps even see in the free spirit a dangerous person. He does so, however, only because his gaze is constricted into one particular epoch of time. If he were able to see beyond it, then he could not but discover at once, that the free spirit has just as little need to transgress the laws of his state as the philistine himself does, and never to set himself in any real opposition to them. For the laws of a state have all sprung from intuitions of free spirits, just as have all other objective moral laws. There is no law enforced by family authority that was not at one time intuitively grasped as such by some ancestor and established by him; the conventional laws of morality are also set up first of all by particular people; and the laws of a state always arise in the head of a statesman. These spirits have set up laws over other people, and only that person becomes unfree, who forgets this origin, and either makes these laws into commandments outside man, into objective moral concepts of duty independent of men, or into the voice of his own inner life, thought of in a falsely mystical way as compelling, which gives him orders. But the person who does not overlook the origin of laws, but rather seeks it within the human being, will relate to a law as though to a part of the same world of ideas out of which he also draws his moral intuitions. If he believes that he has better ones, then his effort is to establish them in the place of existing ones; if he finds the latter to be valid, then he acts according to them as though they were his own.

One may not formulate the principle that the human being is there for the purpose of realizing a moral world order which is separate from him. Whoever were to assert this would still be taking, with respect to the science of man, the same standpoint taken by that natural science which believed that a bull has horns so that it can butt. Scientists, fortunately, have sent this concept of purpose to its grave. Ethics is having more difficulty in freeing itself from this. However, just as horns are not there *because of* butting, but rather butting *through* the horns, so the human being is not there because of morality, but rather morality *through* the human being. The free person acts morally because he has a moral idea; but he does not act so that morality will arise. Human individuals, with their moral ideas belonging to their being, are the prerequisite of a moral world order.

The human individual is the source of all morality and the center of life on earth. State and society are there only because they result necessarily from the life of individuals. That state and society should then work back upon the life of the individual is just as comprehensible as the fact that butting, which is there through horns, works back upon the further development of the bull's horns, which would atrophy through prolonged disuse. In the same way the individual would have to atrophy if he lived a separate life outside of any human community. Indeed, that is exactly why a social order takes shape, in order to work back again upon the individual in a beneficial way.

X
Philosophy of Spiritual Activity and Monism

The naive person, who considers real only what he can see with his eyes and grasp with his hands, also requires for his moral life incentives that are perceptible to the senses. He requires a being who communicates these incentives to him in a way understandable to his senses. He will let these incentives be dictated to him as commandments by a person whom he considers to be wiser and more powerful than himself, or whom, for some other reason, he acknowledges as a power standing over him. There result in this way as moral principles the authorities already enumerated earlier, of family, state, society, church, and divinity. The most limited person still believes in some one other person; the somewhat more advanced person lets his moral behavior be dictated to him by a majority (state, society). Always it is perceivable powers upon which he builds. The person upon whom the conviction finally dawns that these are after all basically just such fallible men as he himself is will seek guidance from a higher power, from a divine being whom he endows with sense-perceptible characteristics. He lets this being again communicate to him the conceptual content of his moral life in a perceivable way, whether it be that God appears in the burning bush, or that He moves about among men in bodily human form and says to them in a way their ears can hear what they ought and ought not to do.

The highest level of development of naive realism in the area of morality is that where the moral commandment (moral idea) is separated from any entity other than oneself, and is hypothetically thought to be an absolute power in one's own inner being. What the human being first perceived as the voice of God from outside, this he now perceives as an independent power in his own inner being, and speaks of this inner voice in such a way that he equates it with his conscience.

With this, however, the level of the naive consciousness is already left behind, and we have entered into the region where the laws of morality are made self-dependent as norms. They then no longer have any bearer, but rather become metaphysical entities that exist in and through themselves. They are analogous to the invisible-visible forces of metaphysical realism, which does not seek reality through the involvement that the human being has with this reality in thinking, but which rather thinks up these forces hypothetically and adds them to what is experienced. Moral norms outside man also always appear in company with this metaphysical realism. This metaphysical realism must also seek the origin of morality in the sphere of some reality outside man. There are different possibilities here. If the assumed being of things is thought of as something essentially without thoughts and as working by purely mechanical laws, which is the picture materialism has of it, then this being will also bring forth the human individual out of itself through purely mechanical necessity, along with everything about him. The consciousness of inner freedom can then only be an illusion. For while I consider myself to be the creator of my action, the matter composing me and its processes of motion are at work within me. I believe myself free; all my actions are, however, actually only results of the material processes underlying my bodily and spiritual organism. Only because we do not know the motives compelling us, do we have the feeling of inner freedom, according to this view. "We must again emphasize here that this feeling of inner freedom . . . rests upon the absence of external compelling motives." "Our actions are necessitated like our thinking." (Ziehen, *Guidelines of Physiological Psychology**)

Another possibility is that a person sees some spiritual being as the absolute, outside man, which exists behind the appearances. Then he will also seek the impulse to action within such a spiritual power. He will regard the moral principles to be found in his reason as flowing from this being-in-itself which has its own particular intentions for man. Moral laws seem, to the dualist of this sort, as though dictated by the absolute, and the human being, through his reason, has simply to discover and carry out the decisions of the absolute being. The moral world

---

**Leitfaden der physiologischen Psychologie.* For the way "materialism" is spoken of here, and the justification for doing so, see the *Addition* to this chapter.

order appears to the dualist to be the perceptible reflection of a still higher order standing behind the moral world order. Earthly morality is the manifestation of a world order outside man. The human being is not the essential thing in this moral order, but rather the being-in-itself, the being outside man. Man *ought* to do what this being *wills*. Eduard von Hartmann, who pictures the being-in-itself as the divinity whose own existence is suffering, believes that this divine being created the world so that through it he might be delivered from his infinitely great suffering. This philosopher, therefore, sees the moral development of mankind as a process which is there in order to deliver the divinity. "Only through the building up of a moral world order by intelligent individuals conscious of themselves, can the world process be led to its goal." "Real existence is the incarnation of the divinity; the world process is the history of the passion of God become flesh, and at the same time the path to the deliverance of the one crucified in the flesh; *morality, however, is our collaboration in the shortening of this path of suffering and deliverance.*" (Hartmann, *Phenomenology of Moral Consciousness**) Here man does not act because he wants to, but rather he *ought* to act, because God wants to be delivered. Just as the materialistic dualist turns man into an automaton, whose actions are only the result of purely mechanical lawfulness, so the spiritual dualist (that is, the person who sees the absolute, the being-in-itself, as a spirituality with which man has no involvement with his conscious experience), turns man into a

Phänomenologie des sittlichen Bewusstseins.

slave to the will of that absolute. Inner freedom, in materialism as well as in one-sided spiritualism, or in any metaphysical realism which infers something outside man as true reality and which does not experience this reality, is out of the question.

Both naive and metaphysical realism, to be consistent, must deny our inner freedom for one and the same reason, because they see in man only the one who executes or carries out principles forced upon him by necessity. Naive realism kills inner freedom through submission to the authority of a perceptible being, or to one conceived of by analogy as perceptible, or, finally, to the abstract inner voice which he *interprets* as "conscience"; the metaphysician who merely infers something outside man cannot acknowledge inner freedom, because he considers man to be mechanically or morally determined by a "being-in-itself."

Monism has to recognize the partial validity of naive realism, because it recognizes the validity of the world of perception. Whoever is incapable of bringing forth moral ideas through intuition must receive them from others. Insofar as man receives his moral principles from outside, he is actually unfree. But monism ascribes to the idea the same significance as to the perception. The idea, however, can come to manifestation within the human individual. Insofar as man follows his impulses from this side, he feels himself to be free. Monism ascribes no validity, however, to the metaphysics which merely draws inferences, nor, consequently, to impulses to action originating from so-called "beings-in-themselves." Man can, according to the monistic view, act unfreely if he follows a perceptible outer compulsion; he can act freely if he obeys only himself. Monism can acknowledge no unconscious compulsion, hidden behind perception and concept. If someone asserts about an action of a fellowman that it is done *unfreely*, then he must show, within the perceptible world, the thing, or the person, or the establishment, which has motivated someone to his action; if the person making this assertion appeals to causes for the action outside of the perceptibly and spiritually real world, then monism cannot enter into such an assertion.

According to the monistic view man acts in part unfreely, in part freely. He finds himself to be unfree in the world of his perceptions, and makes real within himself the *free* spirit.

The moral commandments, which the merely inference-drawing metaphysician has to regard as flowing from a higher power, are, for the believer in monism, *thoughts of men*; the moral world order is for him neither a copy of a purely mechanical natural order, nor of a world order outside man, but rather through and through the free work of man. The human being does not have to accomplish in the world the will of some being lying outside him, but rather his own will; he does not realize the decisions and intentions of another being, but rather his own. Behind the human being who acts, monism does not see the purposes of a world guidance outside himself which determines people according to its will; but rather human beings pursue, insofar as they are realizing intuitive ideas, only their own *human* purposes. And, indeed, each individual pursues his particular purposes. For the world of ideas does not express itself in a community of people, but only in human individuals. What presents itself as the common goal of a whole group of people is only the result of single acts of will by individuals, and usually, in fact, by some chosen few whom the others follow as their authorities. Each of us is called upon to become *a free spirit*, just as each rose seed is called upon to become a rose.

Monism is therefore, in the sphere of truly moral action, a *philosophy of inner freedom*. Because monism is a philosophy of reality, it rejects the metaphysical, unreal restrictions upon the free spirit, just as much as it acknowledges the physical and historical (naive-real). restrictions of the naive person. Because monism does not regard man as a finished product which unfolds its full being at every moment of its life, for monism the dispute as to whether man as such *is free or not* amounts to nothing. Monism sees man as a self-developing being and asks whether, on this course of development, the stage of the free spirit can also be attained.

Monism knows that nature does not release man from her arms already complete as free spirit, but rather that she leads him to a certain stage from which, still as an unfree being, he develops himself further until he comes to the point where he finds himself.

Monism is clear about the fact that a being who acts out of physical or moral compulsion cannot be truly moral. It regards the transition through automatic behavior (according to natural drives and instincts) and through obedient behavior (according to moral norms) as necessary preliminary stages for morality, but sees the possibility of surmounting both transitional stages through the free spirit. Monism frees the truly moral world view in general from the fetters, within the world, of the naive maxims of morality, and from the maxims of morality, outside the world, of the speculative metaphysicians. Monism cannot eliminate the former from the world, just as it cannot eliminate perception from the world, and it rejects the latter because monism seeks within the world all the principles of explanation which it needs to illumine the phenomena of the world, and seeks none outside it. Just as monism refuses even to think about principles of knowledge other than those that exist for men (see pages 113–114), so it also rejects decisively the thought of moral principles other than those that exist for men. Human morality, like human knowledge, is determined by human nature. And just as different beings would understand as knowledge something totally different than we, so different beings would also have a different morality. Morality, for the adherent of monism, is a specifically human characteristic, and *spiritual activity (Freiheit)* the human way to be moral.

First Addendum to the Revised Edition of 1918. A difficulty in judging what has been presented in the two preceding chapters may arise through the fact that one believes oneself to be confronted by a contradiction. On the one hand the experience of thinking is spoken of, which is felt to be of a universal significance equally valid for every human consciousness; on the other hand, the fact has been pointed to here that the ideas which are realized in our moral life and which are of the same nature as the ideas achieved in thinking, express themselves in an individual way in every human consciousness. Whoever feels himself compelled to stop before this confrontation as though before a "contradiction," and whoever does not recognize that precisely in the *living contemplation* of this *actually existing* antithesis a part of the being of man reveals itself, to such a person, neither the idea of knowledge nor that of inner freedom can appear in the right light. For the view which believes its concepts to be merely drawn (abstracted) from the sense world, and which does not allow intuition to come into its own, the thought which is claimed here as a reality will remain a "mere contradiction." For an insight which sees how ideas are intuitively *experienced* as a self-sustaining, real being, the fact becomes clear that man, within the world of ideas surrounding him, lives, *in the act of knowing*, into something which is one for all men, but that, when he borrows from this world of ideas the intuitions for his acts of will, he individualizes a member of this world of ideas *through the same activity* which he unfolds as a universal human activity in the spiritual-ideal process of the act of knowing. What appears to be a logical contradiction—the universal nature of the ideas of knowledge and the individual nature of the ideas of morality—is the very thing which, inasmuch as it is beheld *in its reality*, becomes a living concept. Therein lies a characteristic of man's being, that what is to be intuitively grasped *within man* moves like the living swing of a pendulum, back and forth between universally valid knowledge and individual experience of this universal element. Whoever cannot behold the one end of the pendulum swing in its reality, for him thinking remains only a subjective human activity; whoever cannot grasp the other end, for him, with man's activity in thinking, all individual life seems lost.

For a thinker of the first sort, knowledge, for the other thinker, moral life, is an impenetrable phenomenon. Both will put forward all kinds of things to explain the one or the other, all of which miss the point, because actually the experienceability of thinking is either not grasped by them at all, or is misunderstood to be a merely abstracting activity.

Second Addendum to the Revised Edition of 1918. On pages 162 and 163 materialism is discussed. I am well aware that there are thinkers—such as Th. Ziehen mentioned above—who would not call themselves materialists at all, but to whom, nevertheless, from the point of view presented in this book, this concept must be applied. The point is not whether someone says that for him the world is not restricted to merely material existence; that he is therefore no materialist. The point is rather whether he develops concepts which are applicable *only* to a material existence. Someone who states that "our actions are necessitated like our thinking," has put forward a concept which is applicable merely to material processes, but not to action nor to being; and, if he thought his concept through to the end, he would, in fact, have to think materialistically. That he does not do this results only from that inconsistency which is so often the consequence of thinking which is not carried to its conclusion.—One often hears nowadays that the materialism of the nineteenth century has been done away with scientifically. In actual truth, however, it has not been so at all. It is just that one often does not notice today that one has no ideas other than those with which one can approach only what is material. Materialism cloaks itself now in this way, whereas in the second half of the nineteenth century, it displayed itself openly. The veiled materialism of the present day is no less intolerant toward a view that comprehends the world spiritually than the admitted materialism of the last century. Today's materialism only deceives many people who believe themselves able to reject a spiritually oriented world conception because, after all, the scientific one has "long since left materialism behind."

XI
World Purpose and Life Purpose
(The Vocation of Man)

Among the manifold streams in the spiritual life of mankind, there is one we can follow which may be described as the overcoming of the concept of purpose in realms where it does not belong. *Purposefulness* has its own particular nature within the sequence of phenomena. It is a truly real purposefulness only when, in contrast to the relationship of cause and effect where a preceding event determines a later one, the reverse applies and a subsequent event affects and determines an earlier one. This happens, to begin with, only in the case of human actions. A person carries out an action, which he pictures to himself *beforehand*, and lets himself be moved to his action by this mental picture. What comes later, the action, works with the help of the mental picture upon what comes earlier, the person who acts. This detour through mental picturing is, however, altogether necessary in order for a connection to be purposeful.

In the process which breaks down into cause and effect, the perception is to be distinguished from the concept. The perception of the cause precedes the perception of the effect; cause and effect would simply remain side by side within our consciousness if we were not able to connect them with each other through their corresponding concepts. The perception of the effect can only follow upon the perception of its cause. If the effect is to have a real influence upon the cause, then this can only be through the conceptual factor. For the perceptual factor of the effect is simply not present at all before that of the cause. Whoever maintains that the blossom is the purpose of the root, which means the former has an influence upon the latter, can maintain this only about that factor of the blossom which he can establish through his thinking. The perceptual factor of the blossom has as yet no existence at the time when the root comes into being. For there to be a purposeful connection, however, not merely the ideal lawful connection of the later with the earlier is necessary, but also the concept (the law) of the effect must really, through a perceptible process, influence the cause. A perceptible influence of a concept upon something else, however, we can observe only in human actions. Here alone, therefore, is the concept of purpose applicable. The naive consciousness, which accepts as real only what is perceptible, seeks—as we have repeatedly noted—to transfer something perceptible even into an area where only something ideal is to be known. Within perceptible happenings it seeks perceptible connections, or, if it cannot find such, it *dreams* them up. The concept of purpose valid for subjective actions is an element which lends itself to such dreamed-up connections. The naive person knows how he makes something happen and concludes from this that nature will do it in the same way. Within the purely ideal interconnections of nature he sees not only invisible forces, but also unperceivable real purposes. Man makes his tools to suit his purposes; the naive realist has the Creator build organisms by this same formula. Only quite gradually is this incorrect concept of purpose disappearing from the sciences. In philosophy, even today, it is still up to its mischief in a very harmful way. There people ask about the purpose, outside the world, of the world, about the determinants (and, consequently, about the purpose), outside man, of man, and so on.

Monism rejects the concept of purpose in all areas with the sole exception of human action. It seeks laws of nature, but not purposes of nature. *Purposes of nature* are arbitrary assumptions just as unperceivable forces are (see page 109f.) But also purposes of life which man does not give himself, are unjustified assumptions from the standpoint of monism. Only that is purposeful which man has first made to be so, for only through the realization of an idea does purposefulness arise. The idea, however, becomes operative in the realistic sense only within man. Therefore human life has only the purpose and determination which man gives to it. To the question: What kind of task does man have in life?, monism can only answer: the one which he sets himself. My mission in the world is no predetermined one, but rather it is, at any given moment, the one I choose for myself. I do not enter upon my life's path with fixed marching orders.

Ideas are realized purposefully only through human beings. It is therefore inadmissible to speak of history as the embodiment of ideas. All such expressions as: "History is the development of man toward freedom," or the realization of the moral world order, and so on, are untenable from the monistic point of view.

The adherents of the concept of purpose believe that to give up purpose, they would have to give up all order and unity in the world at the same time. Listen, for example, to Robert Hamerling (*Atomistic Theory of the Will**): "As long as there are *drives* in nature, it is foolishness to deny *purposes* in nature."

"Just as the form of a *limb* of the human body is not determined and controlled by an *idea* of this limb that is hovering somewhere in the air, but rather by its connection with the greater whole, with the body to which the limb belongs, so the form of every being of nature, whether plant, animal, man, is not determined and controlled by an *idea* of the same hovering in the air, but rather by the formal principle of the greater whole of nature which purposefully expresses itself and gives shape to everything." And on page 191 of the same volume: "The theory of purpose maintains only that, *in spite of* the thousand discomforts and sufferings of our creaturely existence, a lofty purposefulness and plan are unmistakably present within the forms and developments of nature—a plan and purposefulness, however, which realize themselves only within the laws of nature, and which cannot aim for some fool's paradise where no death confronts life, and no decay, with all its more or less unpleasing but simply unavoidable intermediary stages, confronts growth."

**Atomistik des Willens*

"When the opponents of the concept of purpose bring a small, laboriously collected rubbish heap of partial or complete, imaginary or real examples showing lack of purpose, against a world full of wonders of purpose such as nature shows in all its realms, then I just find that ludicrous."

What is here called purposefulness? A harmonizing of perceptions into a whole. Since, however, underlying all perceptions, there are laws (ideas), which we find through our thinking, so the systematic harmonizing of the parts of a perceptual whole is, in fact, the ideal harmonizing of the parts of an ideal whole contained within this perceptual whole. The notion that the animal or the human being is not determined by an *idea hovering somewhere in the air*, is all askew, and, when it is set right, the condemned view automatically loses its absurd character. The animal is, to be sure, not determined by an idea hovering somewhere in the air, but is very much determined by an idea which is inborn and which constitutes the lawful nature of its being. Precisely because the idea is not outside the thing, but rather works within it as its very being, one cannot speak of purposefulness. Precisely the person who denies that a being of nature is determined from outside (whether by an idea hovering somewhere in the air, or by an idea existing *outside* the creature in the mind of a world-creator, makes no difference at all in this connection) must admit that this being is not determined purposefully and according to a plan from outside, but rather causally and lawfully from within. I construct a machine purposefully when I bring its parts into a relationship which they do not have by nature. The purposefulness of the arrangement consists then in the fact that I have incorporated the machine's way of working into it as its idea. The machine has become thereby an object of perception with a corresponding idea. The beings of nature are such entities as well. Whoever calls a thing purposeful because it is lawfully formed should then apply this term also to the beings of nature. But this lawfulness should not be confused with that of subjective human actions. For purpose, it is in fact altogether necessary that the cause which is at work be a concept, and indeed the concept of the effect. In nature, however, concepts as causes are nowhere to be found; the concept always shows itself only as the ideal connection of cause and effect. Causes are present in nature only in the form of perceptions.

Dualism can talk about purposes of the world and of nature. Where a lawful joining of cause and effect appears to our perception, there the dualist can assume that we are only seeing the copy of a relationship within which the absolute world being realizes his purposes. For monism, with the falling away of the absolute world being who cannot be experienced but is only hypothetically inferred, there also falls away any reason for ascribing purposes to the world and to nature.

Addendum to the Revised Edition of 1918. If one thinks through without prejudice what has been set forth here, one could not conclude that the author, in his rejection of the concept of purpose outside the human domain, stands on the same ground as those thinkers who, by throwing out this concept, create the possibility of grasping everything which lies outside human actions—and then these also—as *only* a happening of nature. The fact that in this book the thought process is represented as a purely spiritual one should guard against any such conclusion. When here the thought of purpose is also rejected for the *spiritual* world lying outside of human actions, then this is done because in that world something *higher* than the purpose which realizes itself within humanity comes to manifestation. And when a purposeful destiny of the human race, thought up along the lines of human purposefulness, is spoken of as an erroneous idea, then by this is meant that the individual person gives himself purposes and out of these the result of the total activity of mankind is composed. This result is then something higher than its parts, the purposes of men.

XII
Moral Imagination
(Darwinism and Morality)

The *free spirit* acts according to his impulses, that is, according to intuitions chosen from the whole of his world of ideas through thinking. For the *unfree spirit*, the reason he isolates one particular intuition from his world of ideas in order to base an action upon it lies within the world of perceptions given to him, that means within his previous experiences. He remembers, before he comes to a decision, what someone else has done or named as a good thing to do in a case analogous to his own, or what God has dictated in such a case, and so on, and then he acts accordingly. For the free spirit these preconditions are not the only stimulus to action. He makes an absolutely *primal* decision. In doing so, he bothers just as little about what others have done in this case, as about what they have dictated for it. He has purely ideal reasons which move him to lift just one particular concept out of the sum total of his concepts and to translate it into action. His action will, however, belong to perceptible reality. What he brings about will therefore be identical with a quite definite perceptible content. His concept will have to realize itself in a concrete individual happening. It will not, as concept, be able to contain this individual instance. It will be able to relate itself to this only in the way that any concept at all relates itself to a perception; for example, in the way the concept "lion" relates to an individual lion. The intermediary between concept and perception is the *mental picture* (see pages 95–97). For the unfree spirit this intermediary is given from the start. His motives are present from the start as mental pictures in his consciousness. When he wants to carry out an action, he does it in the way he has seen it done or the way he is ordered to do it in this or that case. Authority works therefore best of all through *examples*, that means through providing quite definite single actions for the consciousness of the unfree spirit. The Christian acts less according to the teachings than to the *example* of the Redeemer. Rules have less value for positive action than for leaving certain actions undone. Laws take on the generalized form of concepts only when they forbid actions; not, however, when they order something done. Laws about what he ought to do must be given to the unfree spirit in a quite concrete form: Clean the sidewalk in front of your house! Pay your taxes in this amount at that tax center! and so on. Laws for preventing actions have a conceptual form: You shall *not* steal! You shall *not* commit adultery! These laws also affect the unfree spirit, however, only through reference to some concrete mental picture, for example, to that of the corresponding temporal punishment, or of the pangs of conscience, or of eternal damnation, and so on.

As soon as the stimulus to an action is present in the

generalized form of concepts (for example: You shall do good to your neighbor! You shall live in such a way that you best promote your own welfare!), then in each individual case the concrete mental picture of the action (the relation of the concept to a perceptual content) must first be found. For the *free spirit*, who is not impelled by any example nor by any fear of punishment, etc., this translation of the concept into a mental picture is always necessary.

The human being produces concrete mental pictures out of the sum total of his ideas first of all through imagination. What the free spirit needs in order to realize his ideas, in order to make his way, is therefore *moral imagination.** It is the wellspring for the actions of the free spirit. Therefore, it is also true that only people with moral imagination are actually morally productive. Mere preachers of morality, that is, the people who spin forth moral rules without being able to condense them into concrete mental pictures, are morally unproductive. They are like the art critics who know how to expound judiciously upon the way a work of art ought to be, but who are unable themselves to create even the least little one.

Moral imagination, in order to realize its mental picture, must reach into a particular region of perceptions. Man's action does not create any perceptions, but rather reshapes the perceptions which are already present, imparts to them a new form. In order to be able to reshape a particular object of perception or a number of such, in accordance with a moral mental picture, one must have grasped the lawful content (its way of working until now,

**Moralische Phantasie*

which one wants to shape anew or give a new direction to) of this perceptual configuration. One must furthermore find the method by which this lawfulness allows itself to be transformed into a new one. This part of one's moral activity rests upon knowledge of the phenomenal world with which one is involved. It is therefore to be sought in one branch of scientific knowledge in general. Moral action therefore presupposes, along with the faculty* for moral ideas and along with moral imagination, the ability to transform the world of perceptions without violating their natural lawful connections. This ability is *moral technique.* It can be learned in the same sense that science in general can be learned. Generally, people are in fact better able to find the concepts for the already existing world, than productively, out of their imagination, to determine not yet existing future actions. Hence, it is quite possible that people without moral imagination would receive moral mental pictures from others and would skillfully imprint them upon reality. The opposite case can occur also, that people with moral imagination are without technical skillfulness and must then make use of other people to realize their mental pictures.

Insofar as knowing the objects in our sphere of action is necessary for moral action, our action rests upon this knowing. What comes into consideration here are the *laws of nature.* We have to do with natural science, not with ethics.

---

*Only superficiality could see, in the use of the word "faculty" here and in other places in this book, a relapse into the teachings of an older psychology about faculties of the soul. The connection with what was said on page 85 gives exactly my meaning of the word.

Moral imagination and the capacity for moral ideas can become the object of knowing only *after* they have been produced by the individual. Then, however, they are no longer regulating life, but have already regulated it. They are to be grasped as operating causes like all others (they are purposes merely for the subject). We concern ourselves with them as with a *natural history of moral mental pictures*.

Besides this there can be no ethics as a science of norms.

People have wanted to hold to the normative character of moral laws, at least insofar as they have grasped ethics in the sense of dietetics, which extracts general laws out of the life conditions of the organism, in order then, on the basis of these laws, to influence the body in particular ways (Paulsen, *System of Ethics*★). This comparison is false, because our moral life cannot be compared with the life of our organism. The functioning of the organism is there without our doing; we find all its laws already there in the world, can therefore seek them, and then apply the ones we have found. Moral laws, however, are first *created* by us. We cannot apply them before they are created. The error arises through the fact that moral laws are not created, new in content, at every moment, but rather are handed down to others. The moral laws taken over from our ancestors then appear to be given, like the natural laws of the organism. It will definitely not, however, be as right for future generations to apply them as to apply laws of diet. For moral laws have to do with the individual

★*System der Ethik*

and not, as is the case with a natural law, with a member of a species. As an organism I am just such a member of a species, and I will live in accordance with nature when I apply the natural laws of the species also in my particular case; as a moral being I am an individual and have laws entirely my own.*

The view put forward here seems to stand in contradiction to that basic doctrine of modern natural science known as the *theory of evolution.* But it only *seems* to do so. By *evolution* is understood the *real* emerging of the later out of the earlier in ways corresponding to natural laws. By evolution in the organic world one means that the later (more perfect) organic forms are real descendants of earlier (less perfect) ones, and have emerged from them in a way corresponding to natural laws. The adherents of the theory of organic evolution would actually have to picture to themselves that there was once a period of time on earth when someone could have followed with his eyes the gradual emergence of the reptiles out of the proto-amniotes, if he could have been present as observer back then and had been endowed with sufficiently long life. In the same way the evolutionary theorist would have to picture to himself that a being could have observed the

---

*When Paulsen (on page 15 of the book mentioned above) says that "different natural dispositions and life conditions demand, as well as a different bodily diet, also a different spiritual-moral one," he is very close to the correct view, but still misses the decisive point. Insofar as I am an individual, I need no diet. Dietetics means the art of bringing one particular member into harmony with the general laws of its species. As an individual, however, I am no member of any species.

emergence of the solar system out of the Kant-Laplace primordial nebula, if he had been able to dwell freely in the realm of world ether in a suitable place during that infinitely long time. The fact that, with a picture such as this, both the nature of the proto-amniotes and also that of the Kant-Laplace primordial nebula would have to be thought of *differently* than the materialistic thinkers do, does not come into consideration here. But it should not occur to any evolutionary theorist to maintain that, even without ever having seen a reptile, he could draw forth from his concept of the proto-amniotes that of the reptile with all its characteristics. Just as little could the solar system be deduced from the concept of the Kant-Laplace primordial nebula, if this concept of the primordial nebula is thought of as determined directly only by the perception of the primordial nebula. This means, in other words, that the evolutionary theorist must, if he is consistent in his thinking, maintain that out of earlier phases of development later ones result in a real way, and that, once we have bestowed the concept of less perfect *and* that of perfect, we can then see the connection; by no means, however, should he grant that the concept gained through the earlier is far-reaching enough to evolve the later out of it. From this it follows for the philosopher of ethics that he can in fact gain insight into the connection of later moral concepts with earlier ones; but not that even one single new moral idea can be drawn from an earlier one. As a moral being the individual produces his content. This content he produces is, for the philosopher of ethics, something given, exactly in the same way as, for the scientific researcher, the reptiles are something given.

The reptiles have come forth out of the proto-amniotes; but the scientific researcher cannot draw the concept of the reptiles from that of the proto-amniotes. Later moral ideas evolve out of earlier ones; the philosopher of ethics cannot, however, draw, out of the moral concepts of an earlier cultural epoch, those of later ones. The confusion is caused through the fact that, as scientific researchers, we already have the phenomena before us and only afterward observe and know them; whereas in our moral actions we ourselves first create the phenomena which we then afterward know. In the evolutionary process of the moral world order we do what nature does on a lower level: we transform something perceptible. The ethical norm can therefore at first not *be known* the way a law of nature can, but rather it must be created. Only when it is there can it become the object of our knowing.

But can we not then measure the new against the old? Is not each person compelled to measure what is produced through his moral imagination against the moral teachings already there from the past? For that which is to reveal itself as something morally productive, this is just as nonsensical as it would be for someone to want to measure a new natural form against an old one and then say: Because the reptiles do not match up with the proto-amniotes, they are an invalid (pathological) form.

Ethical individualism does not therefore stand at odds with a rightly understood theory of evolution, but rather follows directly from it. Haeckel's genealogical tree from the protozoa up to man as an organic being would have to be able to be followed, without any break in the lawfulness of nature and without any break in the unity of evo-

lution, right up to the individual as a being who is moral
in a particular sense. At no point, however, could the
nature of a later species be deduced from the *nature* of an
ancestral species. But as true as it is that the moral ideas
of the individual have observably come forth out of those
of his ancestors, it is also just as true that he is morally
barren if he himself does not have any moral ideas.

The same ethical individualism which I have developed on the basis of the preceding considerations could
also be derived out of the theory of evolution. The final
conviction would be the same; only the path upon which
it is achieved would be a different one.

The emergence of totally new moral ideas out of our
moral imagination is, for the theory of evolution, as little
to be wondered at as the emergence of a new species of
animal out of another. But this theory, as a monistic
world view in moral life just as in the life of nature, must
reject any influence from the beyond, any (metaphysical)
influence which is merely inferred and not experienced in
idea. This theory follows thereby the same principle
which motivates it when it seeks the causes of new organic
forms and in so doing does not refer to the intervention of
some being, outside the world, who calls forth each new
species through supernatural influence, according to new
creative thoughts. Just as monism can have no use for any
supernatural creative thoughts to explain a living being,
so for monism it is also impossible to derive the moral
world order from causes which do not lie within the experienceable world. Monism cannot believe that the nature
of an act of will, as a moral one, has been fully explored
by tracing it back to a continuing supernatural influence

upon one's moral life (divine world-rule from outside), or to a particular revelation in time (the giving of the ten commandments), or to the appearance of God (of Christ) on earth. What occurs in and with the human being through all this becomes something moral only when, within his human experience, it becomes something individually his own. For monism the moral processes are produced by the world like everything else that exists, and their causes must be sought *in* the world, that means, in man, because he is the bearer of morality.

Ethical individualism is therefore the crowning feature of that edifice which Darwin and Haeckel have striven to build for natural science. Ethical individualism is spiritualized evolutionary teaching carried over into moral life.

Someone who from the beginning, in a narrow-hearted way, restricts his concept of *nature* to an arbitrarily limited sphere, can easily come to the point of finding no place in nature for free individual action. The evolutionary theorist who proceeds consequently cannot fall into any such narrowness of heart. He cannot terminate natural evolution at the ape and attribute to man a supernatural origin; he must, even when seeking the natural ancestors of man, already seek the spirit in nature; he can also not stop short at the organic functions of man and find only these to be of nature, but rather he must also regard his morally free life as a spiritual continuation of organic life.

According to his basic principles, the evolutionary theorist can only maintain that the moral actions of the present emerge out of other kinds of world happening; his determining of the character of an action, that is whether it is *free*, he must leave up to his *direct observation* of the action. He maintains, after all, only that human beings have evolved out of ancestors that were not yet human. How human beings are constituted must be determined through observation of human beings themselves. The results of this observation cannot come into contradiction with a rightly viewed evolutionary history. Only the assertion that the results are such as to exclude a natural world order could not be brought into agreement with the present direction of natural science.*

Ethical individualism has nothing to fear from a natural science that understands itself: observation shows *inner freedom* to be the characteristic of the perfect form of human action. This freedom must be attributed to human willing, insofar as this willing realizes purely ideal intuitions. For these are not the results of some necessity working upon them from outside, but rather are something based upon themselves. If a person finds that an action is the *image* of such an ideal intuition, he experiences it as a *free* one. In this characteristic of an action lies inner freedom.

How do matters stand now, from this point of view, with the distinction already made above (page 9f. and 4–5) between the two statements: that to be free means to be able to *do* what one wants to, and the other as to whether being at liberty to be able to desire and not to desire is the real proposition involved in the dogma of free will.— Hamerling in fact bases his view about free will upon this

*That we speak of thoughts (ethical ideas) as objects of observation is justified. For even if the configurations of thinking do not also enter into my sphere of observation during my activity of thinking, still, they can become the object of observation afterwards. And in this way we have attained our characterization of the nature of human action.

distinction, in that he declares the first statement to be correct and the second to be an absurd tautology. He says that I can *do* what I want to. But to say that I can want what I want to is an empty tautology.—Whether I can do, that means, can translate into reality, what I want to, what I have therefore put before me as the idea of my doing, this depends upon outer circumstances and upon my technical skill (see page 180f.). To be free means to be able, out of oneself, through moral imagination, to determine which mental pictures (stimuli to action) are to underlie one's actions. Inner freedom is impossible if something outside of me (a mechanical process or a merely inferred God outside the world) determines my moral mental pictures. I am therefore free only when *I* myself produce these mental pictures, not when I *am able* to carry out the stimuli to action which another being has instilled in me. A free being is one that can *want* what he himself considers to be right. Whoever does something other than he wants to, has to be driven to this other thing by motives which do not lie within him. Such a person acts unfreely. To be at liberty to be able to want what one considers to be right or wrong, means therefore to be at liberty to be able to be free or unfree. That is of course just as absurd as to see freedom in the ability to be able to do what one must want. But this last, however, is just what Hamerling maintains when he says that it is perfectly true that the will is always determined by stimuli to action, but that it is absurd to say that the will is therefore unfree; for no greater freedom could either be wished or imagined for it than the freedom to realize itself in proportion to its own strength and determination.—Yes! A greater freedom can indeed be wished for, and only that is the true one; namely, the freedom to determine for oneself the grounds for one's willing.

Under certain circumstances a person may let himself be motivated to refrain from carrying out what he wants to do. To let be prescribed what he *ought to* do, that is, to want what someone else and not he considers to be right, to this he can succumb only insofar as he does not feel himself to be *free*.

External powers can hinder me from doing what I want. They then simply condemn me to doing nothing or to being unfree. Only when they enslave my mind and' spirit and drive my own impulses to action from my head and want to replace them with theirs, do they then intend my inner unfreedom. This is why the church, therefore, works not merely against my *doing*, but especially against my *impure thoughts*, that is against the impulses of my actions. The church makes me unfree if all impulses to action which it does not decree appear impure to it. A church or another community creates inner unfreedom when its priests or teachers make themselves into the ones who dictate conscience, that is, when the faithful *must* draw the impulses for their actions from them (in the confessional).

Addendum to the Revised Edition, 1918. In these considerations of human willing there is presented what the human being can experience with respect to his actions, in order through this experience to come to the consciousness: my willing is free. It is of particular significance that the justification for designating a willing as free is established through the experience that in the willing an ideal intuition realizes itself. This *can* only be the result of observation, but *is* so in the sense in which human willing

observes itself in a stream of development whose goal lies
in reaching just such a potential of willing that is carried
by purely ideal intuitions. This potential can be reached,
because nothing is at work within ideal intuition other
than its own being, which is founded upon itself. If such
an intuition is present in human consciousness, then it
has not developed out of the processes of the organism (p.
133ff.), but rather the organic activity has drawn back, in
order to make room for the ideal activity. If I observe a
willing that is the image of intuition, then the organically
necessary activity has also drawn back out of this willing.
The willing is free. A person will not be able to observe
this freedom of willing who cannot see how free willing
consists in the fact, that *first*, through the intuitive element, the necessary working of the human organism is
paralyzed, forced back, and that the spiritual activity* of
will filled with ideas is set in its place. Only someone who
cannot make *this* observation of the twofold nature of a
free willing believes in the unfreedom of *every* willing.
Whoever can make it struggles through to the insight that
the human being, insofar as he cannot fully accomplish
the process of damming up organic activity, is unfree;
but that this unfreedom is striving toward freedom, and
this freedom is in no way an abstract ideal, but rather is a
power of direction lying within the human being. Man is
free to the extent that he is able in his willing to realize
the same mood of soul which lives in him when he is conscious of giving shape to purely ideal (spiritual) intuitions.

---

*geistige Tätigkeit

XIII
The Value of Life
(Pessimism and Optimism)

A counterpart to the question of the purpose and determinants of life (see page 172ff.) is the question as to its value. We meet two opposing views regarding this, and, in between, every imaginable attempt to reconcile them. One view says that the world is the best imaginable, and that our living and acting in it are a gift of inestimable value. Everything presents itself as a harmonious and purposeful working together and is worthy of wonder. Even what seems to be evil and bad can be recognized from a higher standpoint as good; for it stands there as a beneficial contrast to the good; we can value the latter all the more when it stands out in relief against the former. Furthermore, evil has no true reality; we only experience a lesser degree of the good as evil. Evil is the absence of good; it is nothing that has significance in its own right.

The other view is the one which maintains that life is full of agony and misery, that pain everywhere outweighs pleasure, and suffering everywhere joy. Existence is a burden, and nonexistence would under all circumstances be preferable to existence.

We have to consider Shaftesbury and Leibniz as the main proponents of the first view, of optimism, and Schopenhauer and Eduard von Hartmann as those of the second view, of pessimism.

Leibniz believes that the world is the best that could possibly be. A better one is impossible. For God is good and wise. A good God *wants* to create the best of worlds; a wise God *knows* the best; He can distinguish the best world from all other possible worse ones. Only an evil or unwise God could create a world worse than the best possible.

Whoever takes this view as his starting point will easily be able to prescribe the direction our human actions must take in order that they contribute what they can to the best of worlds. The human being has only to discover what God's ways are for him and then act accordingly. When he knows what God's intentions are for the world and for the human race, then he will also do the right thing. And he will feel happy in adding also his good to the general good. From the optimistic standpoint life is therefore worth living. It must stimulate us to coactive involved participation.

Schopenhauer pictures the matter differently. He does not think of the ground of existence as an all-wise and all-good being, but rather as blind urge or will. Eternal striving, ceaseless craving for a satisfaction which can never in fact be attained, is the basic thrust of all willing. For when we have attained one of the goals we have striven for, there arises a fresh need and so on. Any satisfaction can only last for an infinitely small time. All the rest of the content of our life is unsatisfied urge, that is, discontent, suffering. If our blind urges are finally dulled, then we lack any content; an endless boredom fills our existence. Therefore the relatively best thing to do is to stifle the wishes and needs within us, to extinguish our willing. Schopenhauer's pessimism leads to inaction; his moral goal is *universal laziness*.

Hartmann seeks in a considerably different way to establish pessimism and to make use of it in ethics. Hartmann seeks, in keeping with a favorite tendency of our day, to found his world view upon *experience*. By observing life he wants to determine whether pleasure or pain* outweighs the other in the world. He lets pass in review before reason what seems good and satisfying to people, in order to show that all this supposed gratification proves, upon closer inspection, to be *illusion*. It is illusion when we believe ourselves to have sources of happiness and satisfaction in health, youth, freedom, adequate livelihood, love (sexual enjoyment), compassion, friendship and family life, self-respect, honor, fame, power, religious edification, scientific and artistic pursuits, expectation of life in the beyond, and participation in cultural progress. When looked at soberly, every enjoyment brings far more evil and misery than pleasure into the world. *The unpleasantness of the hangover is always greater than the pleasant feeling of intoxication.* Pain predominates in the world by far. No man, even the relatively happiest one, if asked, would want to go through this miserable life a second

---

Die Lust oder die Unlust.

time. But now, since Hartmann does not deny the presence of the ideal (of wisdom) in the world, grants it in fact equal standing with blind urge (will), he can credit his primal Being with the creation of the world only if he traces the pain of the world back to a wise world purpose. The pain of the cosmic Being is, however, none other than the pain of God Himself, for the life of the world as a whole is identical with the life of God. An all-wise Being can only see His goal, however, to be in the release from suffering, and since all existence is suffering, in the release from existence. To lead existence over into non-existence, which is far better, is the purpose of the creation of the world. The world process is a continuous battle against God's pain, finally leading to the eradication of all existence. The moral life of men becomes therefore participation in the eradication of existence. God has created the world so that through it He can free Himself from His infinite pain. This world is "to be regarded in a certain way as an itching eruption upon the absolute Being," through which His unconscious healing power frees Him from an internal illness, "or even as a painful poultice which the All-One-Being applies to Himself, in order first to divert an inner pain outward and then to cast it off." Human beings are parts of the world. Within them God suffers. He has created them in order to split up this infinite pain. The pain which each one of us suffers is only a drop in the infinite ocean of God's pain (Hartmann, *Phenomenology of Moral Consciousness*).

Man has to permeate himself with the knowledge that the pursuit of individual gratification (egoism) is folly, and he has to let himself be guided solely by the task of dedicating himself with selfless devotion to the world process of God's deliverance. The pessimism of Hartmann, in contrast to that of Schopenhauer, leads us to devoted activity on behalf of a lofty task.

But is all this based on experience?

Striving for gratification is a reaching out of one's life activity beyond the present content of life. A being is hungry; i.e., it strives to fill itself, when its organic functions demand new life content in the form of nourishment in order to continue. The striving for honor consists in the fact that a person considers what he himself does or refrains from doing, worthwhile only when recognition from outside follows his actions. The striving for knowledge arises when something is lacking for a person in the world he sees, hears, etc., for as long as he has not comprehended it. The success of his striving creates pleasure in the striving individual; its failure creates pain. It is important to note in this that pleasure or pain depend only upon the success or failure of my striving. The striving itself can in no way be accounted as pain. If it turns out, therefore, that in the moment one's striving is realized, another one presents itself right away, I still cannot say that pleasure has given birth to pain for me just because enjoyment always creates desire that it be repeated or desire for new pleasure. Only when this desire hits up against the impossibility of its being satisfied, can I speak of pain. Even in the case where an enjoyment I have experienced creates in me the demand for a greater or more refined experience of pleasure, I can speak of pain being created by the first pleasure only at the moment when the means fail me for experiencing the greater or more refined pleasure. Only in the case where pain occurs as a naturally lawful result of pleasure, as for example when the woman's sexual enjoyment results in the sufferings of childbirth and in the cares of rearing children, can I find in enjoyment the creator of pain. If striving in itself called forth pain, then any removal of striving would have to be accompanied by pleasure. The opposite is, however, the case. A lack of striving in the content of our life creates boredom, and this brings pain with it. But since striving, in the nature of things, can last for a long time before success is granted it and is content meanwhile with its hope for this success, so it must be recognized that pain has absolutely nothing to do with striving as such, but rather depends on its non-fulfillment alone. Schopenhauer is therefore in any case wrong when he considers desire and striving (will) in themselves to be the source of pain.

In fact, just the opposite is correct. Striving (desire) in itself creates joy. Who does not know the enjoyment which the hope brings of reaching a distant but strongly desired goal? This joy is the companion of work whose fruits will only be forthcoming to us in the future. This pleasure is entirely independent of our reaching the goal. When the goal is reached, then to the pleasure of striving, the pleasure of its fulfillment is added as something new. But if someone wanted to say that to the pain of not reaching one's goal there is added also the pain of disappointed hope which in the end makes the pain of unfulfillment still greater, one would answer him that the opposite can also be the case; the looking back on the enjoyment of the time of unfulfilled desire will just as often work to ease the pain of unfulfillment. The person who in the face of his dashed hopes calls out, "I have done all I can!" is living proof of this assertion. The happiness of feeling that one has striven to do the best one could is overlooked by those who maintain about each unrealized desire that not only is the joy of fulfillment unforthcoming, but also that the enjoyment of desiring is itself destroyed.

Fulfillment of desire calls forth pleasure and its unfulfillment, pain. One may not infer from this that pleasure is the satisfying of desire and pain the non-satisfying of desire. Both pleasure and pain can occur in a being, even without their being the result of desire. Illness is pain unpreceded by desire. Someone who wanted to maintain that illness is unsatisfied desire for health would be making the mistake of considering as a positive desire the wish, quite natural but not brought to consciousness, not to become ill. If someone receives an inheritance from a wealthy relative of whose existence he had not had the slightest inkling, this fact still fills him with pleasure without any desire preceding it.

Whoever therefore wants to investigate whether there is a predominance on the side of pleasure or on the side of pain must take into account the pleasure in desiring, the pleasure in the fulfillment of desire, and the pleasure that comes to us unsought. Onto the debit side of the ledger will have to be entered the pain of boredom, the pain of unfulfilled striving, and finally the pain that comes our way without any desire on our part. To the last category belongs also the pain caused by work forced upon us, not of our choosing.

The question arises now as to the right means of determining, from the *debit* and the *credit* side, what our *balance* is. Eduard von Hartmann is of the opinion that it is our reason which does this, in its ability to weigh things up. He says indeed (*Philosophy of the Unconscious**): "Pain and pleasure *exist* only insofar as they are *experienced.*" It follows from this that there is no other yardstick for pleasure than the subjective one of feeling. I must *experience* whether the sum total of my feelings of pain, when put beside my feelings of pleasure, show a predominance in me of joy or pain. In spite of this Hartmann asserts, "Although . . . the life-value of each being can only be assessed according to its own subjective yardstick . . . , this in no way says that each being, out of all the feelings in his life, can find the *correct* algebraic balance, or, in other words, that *his overall judgment* of his own life with respect to his subjective experiences is a correct one." But this still makes *rational judgment* of our feeling into the evaluator.**

Whoever adheres more or less exactly to the way such thinkers as Eduard von Hartmann picture things, can believe that, in order to come to a correct evaluation of life, he must clear out of his way those factors which falsify our *judgment* as to the balance between pleasure and pain. He can seek to achieve this in two ways. *Firstly*,

---

**Philosophie des Unbewussten*

**Whoever wants to *calculate* whether the sum total of pleasure or that of pain outweighs the other ignores the fact that he is undertaking a calculation of something that is nowhere experienced. Feeling does not calculate, and for the real evaluation of life, it is a matter of real experience, and not of the result of a calculation someone has dreamed up.

by showing that our desire (drive, will) acts disruptively upon our sober judging of a feeling's value. Whereas, for example, we would have to say that sexual pleasure is a source of evil, still the fact that the sex drive is powerful in us misleads us into conjuring up before us a pleasure which is absolutely not there to that degree. We want to enjoy; therefore we do not admit to ourselves that we suffer under our pleasures. *Secondly,* by subjecting his feelings to critical judgment and by seeking to show that the objects to which his feelings attach themselves prove before rational knowledge to be illusions, and *that they are destroyed the moment our ever-growing intelligence sees through the illusions.*

He can think the matter through for himself in the following way. If an ambitious person wants to make clear to himself whether, up to the moment of making this calculation, pleasure or pain had had the greater part in his life, then he must free himself in this evaluation from two sources of error. Since he is ambitious, this basic feature of his character will show him his joys from the recognition of his accomplishments through a magnifying glass but will show him his hurt at being slighted, through a glass which makes things look smaller. Back when he experienced the slights, he felt the hurt, precisely because he is ambitious; to memory it appears in a milder light, whereas the joys of recognition, for which he is so receptive, imprint themselves all the more deeply. Now for the ambitious person it is truly a blessing that this is so. Delusion lessens his feeling of pain in the moment of self-observation. Nevertheless his assessment is still an incorrect one. The sufferings, over which a veil is

now drawn for him, had really to be gone through in all
their intensity, and he therefore enters them, in fact, in-
correctly into the account book of his life. In order to
come to a correct estimate, the ambitious person would
have to free himself, during the time of his self-assessment,
from his ambition. He would have to look, without any
kind of glass in front of his spiritual eye, upon his life until
now. Otherwise he is like a merchant who, in making up
his books, enters onto the credit side his own business
zeal as well.

He can, however, go still further. He can say that the
ambitious person will also have to make clear to himself
that the recognition he pursues is a worthless thing. He
will himself come to the insight, or be brought to it by
other people, that to an intelligent person the recognition
of men means nothing, since in fact, "in all such matters,
other than questions of sheer existence, or that are not
already definitively settled by science," one can always
swear by it "that the majority is wrong and the minority
right." "It is into the hands of such judgment that a person puts his life's happiness when he makes ambition his
guiding star." (*Philosophy of the Unconscious*) If the ambitious person does say all this to himself, then he must
label as illusion what his ambition has pictured to him as
reality, and consequently also the feelings which are connected with the particular illusions of his ambition. For
this reason it could then be said that in the ledger of what
has value in life, there have still to be deleted the feelings
of pleasure connected with illusions; what then is left represents the sum total, free of illusion, of the pleasure one
has had in life, and this, compared with the amount of

pain in life, is so small that life is joyless, and non-existence preferable to existence.

But while it is immediately intelligible that the error, caused by the interference of ambition's drive, in figuring out one's pleasure-balance, brings about an incorrect result, what was said about one's knowledge of the illusory nature of the objects of one's pleasure must still be challenged. To exclude from one's pleasure-balance in life all feelings of pleasure connected with actual or supposed illusions would in fact render this balance incorrect. For, the ambitious person genuinely did enjoy his recognition by the masses, quite irrespective of whether he himself, or someone else, afterwards knows this recognition to be an illusion. The happy feeling he enjoyed is not thereby decreased at all. The exclusion of all such "illusory" feelings from our life-balance definitely does not correct our judgment about our feelings, but rather eliminates from our life feelings which were actually present.

And why should these feelings be excluded? For the person who has them they are in fact pleasurable; for the person who has overcome them, there arises through the experience of overcoming (not through the self-complacent experience of what a great person I am, but rather through the objective source of pleasure that lies in overcoming) a pleasure, spiritualized, to be sure, but not thereby less significant. If feelings are deleted from our pleasure-balance because they adhere to objects which turn out to be illusions, then the value of life is made dependent not upon the amount of pleasure, but rather upon the quality of pleasure, and this in turn upon the value of the things which cause the pleasure. But if I want first of all to deter-

mine the value of life according to the amount of pleasure
or pain which it brings me, then I must not presuppose
something else through which I first determine the value
or non-value of the pleasure. If I say that I want to compare the amount of pleasure to the amount of pain and to
see which is greater, then I must also take into account all
pleasure and pain in their actual magnitude, quite irrespective of whether they are based on illusion or not.
Whoever attributes a lesser value for life to a pleasure
based on illusion than to one which can justify itself to
reason, makes the value of life in fact dependent upon
still other factors than upon pleasure.

Whoever attaches less value to a pleasure because it is
connected with a frivolous object is like a merchant who
enters the considerable income from his toy factory into
his accounts at a quarter of its actual amount because his
factory produces playthings for children.

When it is merely a matter of weighing an amount of
pleasure against an amount of pain, then the illusory
nature of the objects of certain feelings of pleasure should
therefore be left entirely out of the picture.

The way Hartmann has suggested for looking intelli-
gently at the amounts of pleasure and pain caused by life
has therefore led us far enough now to know how we have
to set up our calculations, what we have to enter on the
one side of our ledger and what on the other. But how is
the calculation now to be made? And is our reason quali-
fied to determine the balance?

A merchant has made an error in his calculations if his
calculated profit does not agree with what the business actually has taken in or still will take in. A philosopher also

will definitely have made an error in his assessment, if he cannot show that the surplus of pleasure, or of pain as the case may be, which he has somehow reasoned out, does actually exist in our feeling.

I do not for the moment want to monitor the calculations of the pessimists who base themselves upon a rational consideration of the world; but a person who has to decide whether he should go on with the business of life or not will first demand to be shown where the calculated surplus of pain is to be found.

Here we have touched the point where reason is *not* in a position to determine by itself alone any surplus of pleasure or pain, but rather where reason must show this surplus to be a perception in life. Not in the concept alone, but rather in the interweaving, by means of thinking, of concept and perception (and feeling is a perception) is reality accessible to man (see page 77ff.). The merchant also will in fact give up his business only when the losses which his bookkeeper has recorded are confirmed by the facts. If that is not the case, he asks his bookkeeper to make the calculation over again. And that is exactly the same way a person standing in life will do it. When the philosopher tries to show him that pain is far greater than pleasure, but he does not experience it that way, then he will say to the philosopher: You, in your delvings, have made a mistake; think the matter through once more. But if at a certain point in a business such losses are actually present to the extent that there is not enough on the credit side to satisfy the creditors, then bankruptcy occurs if the merchant has failed to maintain clarity about his affairs through keeping accounts. In just the same way it would have to lead to a bankruptcy in the business of life, if the amount of pain became so great for a person at a given moment, that no hope (credit) of future pleasure could get him over the pain.

Now the number of suicides, however, is a relatively small one compared to the number of people who courageously go on living. Very few people close down the business of life because of existing pain. What can we conclude from this? Either that it is not correct to say that the amount of pain is greater than that of pleasure, or that we do not at all make our continued existence dependent upon the amount of pleasure or pain we experience.

The pessimism of Eduard von Hartmann comes in a very peculiar manner to the point of declaring life worthless, because pain predominates in it, but of maintaining nevertheless the necessity of undergoing it. This necessity lies in the fact that the purpose of the world described above (p. 195ff.) can only be attained through the ceaseless devoted work of men. As long as men are still pursuing their own egoistic desires, however, they are unsuited for such selfless work. Only when they have convinced themselves through experience and reason that the pleasures in life striven for by egoism cannot be attained, will they devote themselves to their actual task. In this way the pessimistic persuasion is supposed to be the source of selflessness. An education based on pessimism is supposed to eradicate egoism through demonstrating its hopelessness.

According to this view therefore the striving for pleasure is originally founded in human nature. Only out of insight into the impossibility of fulfillment does this striving withdraw and make way for higher human tasks.

It cannot be said of the moral world view which hopes through the recognition of pessimism for a devotion to unegoistical goals in life, that it overcomes egoism in the true sense of the word. It supposes that moral ideals will only then be strong enough to master the will, when man has recognized that selfish striving for pleasure cannot lead to satisfaction. The person whose self-seeking craves the grapes of pleasure declares them to be sour because he cannot reach them: he leaves them and devotes himself to a selfless transformation of his life. Moral ideals, in the opinion of the pessimists, are not strong enough to overcome egoism; but rather they set up their rulership upon the ground cleared for them beforehand by knowledge of the hopelessness of self-seeking.

If men, out of their natural predisposition, strive after pleasure, but cannot possibly attain it, then annihilation of existence and deliverance through non-existence would be the only rational goal. And if one is of the view that God is the actual bearer of the pain of the world, then human beings would have to make it their task to bring about the deliverance of God. The attainment of this goal is not helped by the suicide of the individual person, but rather harmed by it. Rationally, God can only have created human beings so that through their actions they could bring about His deliverance. Otherwise the creation would be purposeless. And such a world view does think in terms of purposes outside man. Each person must carry out his particular part in the general work of deliverance. If he evades his task through suicide, then the work intended for him must be done by someone else. The latter must bear the torment of existence instead of him. And since God is in every being as the actual bearer of his pain, the suicide has not lessened at all the amount of God's pain, rather, he has imposed the new difficulty upon God of creating a replacement for him.

All this presupposes that pleasure is the yardstick for the value of life. Life manifests itself in a sum of drives (needs). If the value of life depended upon whether it brings more pleasure or pain, then a drive must be designated as worthless which causes its bearer a surplus of the latter. Let us look now at drive and pleasure to see whether the first can be measured by the second. In order not to arouse the suspicion that we believe life to begin only in the sphere of the "aristocracy of the mind," let us begin with a "purely animal" need, hunger.

Hunger arises when our organs can no longer continue their proper function unless new substance is given them. What the hungry person seeks first of all is to eat enough. As soon as enough food has been taken in for hunger to cease, then everything has been achieved which the drive to be fed seeks. The enjoyment connected with eating enough consists first of all in removing the pain which hunger causes. To this drive merely to be fed, there comes another need. A person does not merely want, through taking in nourishment, to restore the normal functioning of his organs, or, as the case may be, to still the pain of hunger: he seeks to effect this to the accompaniment of pleasant taste sensations. When he is hungry and a meal promising rich enjoyment is a half hour away, he can even avoid spoiling his pleasure in the better food by not eating something inferior which could satisfy him sooner. He needs his hunger in order to have the full enjoyment of his meal. Through this, hunger becomes for him a cause of pleasure at the same time. If now all the hunger present in the world could be stilled, this would result in the total amount of enjoyment which we owe to the existence of our need for food. Still to be added to this is the particular enjoyment aimed at by gourmets through a cultivation of the palate beyond the ordinary.

This amount of enjoyment would have the greatest conceivable value when no need, aiming at the kind of enjoyment now under consideration, remained unsatisfied, and when along with the enjoyment a certain amount of pain did not have to be taken into the bargain at the same time.

Modern science holds the view that nature produces more life than it can sustain, which means that it also brings forth more hunger than it is in a position to satisfy. The excess life that is produced must perish painfully in the struggle for existence. Admittedly: the needs of living things at every moment of the world process are greater than the means existing to meet and satisfy them, and this does detract from life's enjoyment. The individual enjoyment actually present in life, however, is not made the least bit smaller. Wherever the satisfying of a desire occurs, the corresponding amount of enjoyment is then present, even though there are still a great number of unsatisfied drives as well within the desiring being itself or in others. But what is diminished thereby is the *value* of the enjoyment of life. If only a part of the needs of a living thing are satisfied, then this being has a corresponding enjoyment. This enjoyment has a lesser value the smaller it is in proportion to the total demands of life in the areas of the desires in question. One can think of this value as represented by a fraction, whose numerator is the enjoyment actually present and whose denominator is the sum total of need. The fraction has the value 1 when numerator and denominator are the same, that means, when all needs are also satisfied. It will be greater than 1 when in a living creature more pleasure is present than its desires demand; and it is less than 1 when the amount of enjoyment lags behind the sum of its desires. The fraction can never reach *zero*, however, as long as the numerator has even the smallest value. If a person, before his death, were to close his accounts, and were to imagine the amount of enjoyment accruing to one particular drive (to hunger, for example) dispersed over his whole life with all the demands of this drive, the pleasure he experienced would perhaps have only little value; but it can never become totally valueless. If the amount of enjoyment of a living creature remains the same while its needs increase, then the value of its pleasure in life diminishes. The same is true for the sum total of all life in nature. The greater the number of living creatures is in relation to the number of those that can fully satisfy their drives, the smaller is the average pleasure-value of life. The bills of exchange that are drawn for us in our drives with respect to our enjoyment of life decrease in value if one cannot expect them to be honored at their full value. If for three days I have enough to eat but then must go hungry the next three days, the enjoyment of the days on which I ate does not become less thereby. But I must then picture it to myself as apportioned over six days, whereby its *value* for my drive to eat is reduced by half.

The situation is the same for the amount of pleasure in relation to the *degree* of my need. If I have enough appetite for two pieces of bread and can only have one, then the enjoyment I derive from the one has only half the value that it would have if I were fully satisfied after eating. This is the way that the *value* of a pleasure is determined in life. Pleasure is measured against the needs of life. Our desires are the *yardstick*; pleasure is what is measured. Value is attached to the pleasure of eating enough only through the fact that hunger is present; and the value attached is of a particular degree through the relationship in which it stands to the degree of hunger present.

The unfulfilled demands of our life cast their shadows even upon desires which have been satisfied, and detract from the *value* of hours filled with enjoyment. But one can also speak of the *present value* of a feeling of pleasure. This value is all the smaller, the less our pleasure is in relation to the duration and intensity of our desire.

An amount of pleasure has full value for us which in duration and degree matches our desire exactly. A smaller amount of pleasure, compared to our desire, reduces the pleasure-value; a greater amount creates an unasked for excess, which is experienced as pleasure only as long as we are able, while enjoying it, to intensify our desire. If we are not in a position to keep step, in the intensifying of our demands, with the increasing pleasure, then the pleasure turns into pain. The object which otherwise would be satisfying to us storms in upon us without our wanting it, and we suffer under it. This is one proof of the fact that pleasure is of value to us only so long as we can measure it against our desire. An excess of pleasurable feeling veers over into pain. We can observe this particularly with people whose demands for one kind of pleasure or another are very small. For people whose drive to eat is dulled, eating can easily become repugnant. It follows from this also, that desire is what measures the value of pleasure.

Now the pessimist could say that the unsatisfied drive to eat brings not only the pain of lost enjoyment, but also positive suffering, agony, and misery into the world. He can cite here the unspeakable misery of those suffering want, and the amount of pain which springs for such people indirectly through the lack of food. And if he wants to apply his assertion also to nature outside man, he can point to the agonies of the animals that starve from lack of food at certain times of the year. Of these evils the pessimist maintains that they far outweigh the amount of enjoyment which our drive to eat brings into the world.

There is indeed no doubt that one can compare *pleasure* and *pain* with each other and can determine the excess of one over the other, as this is done in *profit* and *loss*. But if the pessimist believes that an excess occurs on the side of pain, and believes he can infer from this that life has no value, then he is already in error, insofar as he is making a calculation which is not carried out in real life.

Our desire directs itself in a given case toward a particular object. The pleasure-value of its satisfaction, as we have seen, will be the greater, the greater the amount of pleasure is in relation to the intensity of our desire.★ But

---

★We disregard here the instance where, through excessive increase, pleasure veers over into pain.

it also depends upon the intensity of our desire, how great the amount of pain is which we are willing to take into the bargain in order to attain the pleasure. We compare the amount of pain, not with that of pleasure, but rather with the intensity of our desire. Someone who takes great joy in eating will, because of his enjoyment during better times, more easily get himself through a period of hunger, than will someone else who lacks this joy in satisfying his drive to eat. The woman who wants to have a child does not compare the pleasure which possessing the child affords her with the amount of pain resulting from pregnancy, childbirth, child care, and so on, but rather with her desire for having the child.

We never strive after an abstract pleasure of a particular intensity, but rather after concrete satisfaction in a very definite way. When we are striving for a pleasure which must be afforded by one particular object or by one particular sensation, then we cannot be satisfied by being given a different object or a different sensation that affords us a pleasure of the same intensity. With someone whose aim is to satisfy his hunger, one cannot replace the pleasure of doing so with one equally as great but caused by a walk. Only if our desire strove quite generally for a particular quantity of pleasure would it then have to grow silent at once if this pleasure were not attainable without a quantity of pain surpassing it in intensity. But since satisfaction is striven for in a particular way, pleasure still accompanies fulfillment even when pain greater than it has to be taken into the bargain along with it. Through the fact that the drives of living creatures move in a definite direction and go straight toward a concrete goal, the possibility ceases of bringing into our calculations, as a factor of equal validity, the amount of pain that has set itself in the way to this goal. When the pain is overcome—however great it might be—and the desire is still strong enough to be present to any degree at all, then the pleasure of satisfaction can still be savored in its full intensity. Desire, therefore, does not bring pain directly into relation with the pleasure attained, but rather indirectly in that it brings its own intensity (comparatively) into relation with the pain. It is not a matter of whether the pleasure to be attained or the pain is greater, but rather of whether the desire for the goal striven for or the resistance of the pain opposing it is greater. If this resistance is greater than the desire, then the latter gives way to the inevitable, slackens, and strives no further. Through the fact that satisfaction is demanded in a definite way, the pleasure connected to it gains a significance which makes it possible, after the satisfaction has occurred, to take the necessary quantity of pain into account only insofar as it has decreased the measure of our desire. If I am passionately fond of views, then I never calculate how much pleasure the view from a mountain peak brings me compared directly with the pain of the laborious ascent and descent. I do, however, consider whether my desire for the view, after overcoming the difficulties, will still be lively enough. Only indirectly through the intensity of the desire can pleasure and pain, when compared, give a result. It is absolutely not a question, therefore, of whether pleasure or pain is present to a greater extent, but whether the wanting of the pleasure is strong enough to overcome the pain.

A proof of the correctness of this view is the fact that

the value of a pleasure is rated more highly when it has to be purchased at the price of great pain, than when it falls into our lap, as it were, like a gift from heaven. When pain and suffering have toned down our desire and then the goal is still reached after all, the pleasure, *in relation* to the quantity of desire still remaining, is all the *greater*. But this relation represents, as I have shown, the *value* of the pleasure (see page 208ff.). A further proof is given through the fact that living creatures (including man) unfold their drives as long as they are able to bear the pain and suffering which oppose them. And the struggle for existence is only the result of this fact. Existing life strives to unfold itself and only that part gives up the struggle whose desires are stifled through the force of the difficulties rising up against them. Every living thing keeps seeking food until lack of food destroys its life. And even man turns his hand against himself only when he believes (rightly or wrongly) that he cannot attain the goals in life which seem to him worth striving for. But as long as he still believes in the possibility of attaining what in his view is worth striving for, he will struggle on against all suffering and pain. Philosophy would first have to impose upon the human being the view that willing makes sense only when pleasure is greater than pain; by nature he wants to attain the objects of his desire if he can bear whatever pain becomes necessary in doing so, be it ever so great. Such a philosophy would be in error, however, because it makes human willing dependent upon a condition (excess of pleasure over pain) which is to begin with foreign to man. The primal yardstick of willing is desire, and desire presses forward as long as it can. One can compare the calculation, which *life*, not an intellectual philosophy, makes, when it is a question of pleasure and pain in satisfying a desire, with the following. If, when buying a certain quantity of apples, I am forced to take twice as many bad ones as good ones—because the seller wants to clear out his stock—then I will not think twice about taking the bad apples as well if I can value the smaller amount of good ones highly enough that along with the selling price I also still want to take upon myself the expense of disposing of the bad wares. This example illustrates the relation between the amounts of pleasure and pain caused by a drive. I determine the value of the good apples, not by subtracting their number from that of the bad ones, but by whether the former still retain some value despite the presence of the latter.

Just as, in my enjoyment of the good apples, I leave the bad ones out of account, so I give myself over to the satisfaction of a desire after I have shaken off the unavoidable pain.

Even if pessimism were right in its assertion that more pain than pleasure is present in the world, this would have no influence upon our willing, for in spite of this, living creatures strive for whatever pleasure is left. Empirical proof that pain outweighs joy, if it could be provided, would indeed be able to show the futility of that philosophical direction which sees the value of life in an excess of pleasure (eudaemonism), but it could not show willing in general to be irrational, for willing does not pursue an excess of pleasure but rather the amount of pleasure still left over after the pain is discounted. This still appears as a goal worth striving for.

One has tried to refute pessimism by maintaining that it is impossible to calculate an excess of pleasure or pain in the world. The possibility of any kind of calculation depends upon the fact that the things to be calculated can be compared with each other in magnitude. Now every pain and every pleasure has a definite magnitude (intensity and duration). Pleasurable sensations of different kinds can also be compared with each other, at least approximately, according to magnitude. We know whether a good cigar or a good joke gives us more pleasure. Against the comparability of different kinds of pleasure and pain, according to magnitude, there can thus be no objections raised. And the researcher who makes it his task to determine an excess of pleasure or pain in the world takes his start from presuppositions which are altogether justified. One can maintain that the results of pessimism are in error, but one cannot doubt either the possibility of a scientific estimation of the amounts of pleasure and pain, nor that a pleasure balance can thereby be determined. It is, however, incorrect if someone maintains that the results of this calculation have any consequences for human willing. The instances where we make the value of our actions really dependent upon whether pleasure or pain shows itself to exceed the other, are those in which the objects to which we direct our actions are indifferent to us. If it is a matter, after work, of my enjoying myself with a game or in light conversation, and I am completely indifferent as to what I do for this purpose, then I ask myself what will give me the greater pleasure. And I definitely refrain from an activity if the scale dips toward the side of pain. With a child for whom we want to buy a toy, we think, in making our choice, about what will give him the most pleasure. In all other instances we do not go exclusively by the balance of pleasure.

When therefore the pessimistic philosophers of ethics are of the view that by showing pain to be present in greater quantity than pleasure they prepare the ground for selfless devotion to the task of civilization, they do not bear in mind that human willing does not by its nature let itself be influenced by such knowledge. The striving of men directs itself toward the measure of satisfaction possible after all difficulties are overcome. The hope of this satisfaction is the basis of human activity. The work of every single person and all the work of civilization springs from this hope. Pessimistic ethics believes it must represent the pursuit of happiness to man as an impossible one, so that he will dedicate himself to his real moral tasks. But these moral tasks are nothing other than his concrete natural and spiritual drives; and the satisfaction of these is striven for in spite of the pain that falls to him thereby. The pursuit of happiness which pessimism wants to eradicate is therefore not present at all. But the tasks which man has to fulfill, he fulfills, because, by virtue of his nature, when he has really known their nature, he *wants* to fulfill them. Pessimistic ethics maintains that man will be able to devote himself to what he recognizes to be his life's task only when he has given up his striving for pleasure. No ethics, however, can ever conceive life tasks other than the realization of those satisfactions demanded by human desires and the fulfillment of his moral ideals. No ethics can take away from him the pleasure he has in this fulfillment of what he desires.

When the pessimist says: Do not strive for pleasure, for you can never attain it; strive for what you recognize as your task; then the reply to this is: That is human nature, and it is the invention of a philosophy going off on false paths when it is asserted that man strives merely for happiness. He strives for the satisfaction of what his being desires, and he has his eye upon the concrete objects of this striving, not upon some abstract "happiness"; this fulfillment is a pleasure for him. When pessimistic ethics demands a striving not for pleasure, but rather for the attainment of what one recognizes as one's life's task, it hits upon the very thing that man by nature *wants*. The human being does not need to first be turned topsy-turvy by philosophy, he does not need first to cast off his nature in order to be moral. Morality lies in striving for a goal that one recognizes as justified; it lies in man's being to pursue this goal, as long as the pain connected with it does not lame the desire for it. And this is the nature of all real willing. Ethics is not based upon the eradication of all striving for pleasure so that anemic, abstract ideas can establish their rule there where no strong longing for enjoyment of life opposes them; but rather, it is based upon *strong willing*, carried by ideal intuition, that reaches its goal even though the path to it is a thorny one.

Ethical ideals spring from the moral imagination of man. Their realization depends upon their being desired by a person strongly enough to overcome pain and suffering. They are *his* intuitions, the mainsprings that his spirit winds; he *wills* them, because their realization is his highest pleasure. It is not necessary for him first to let himself be forbidden by ethics to strive after pleasure in order then to let himself be told what *ought* to be the goal of his striving. He will strive after ethical ideals if his moral imagination is active enough to inspire him with intuitions that grant his willing the strength to make its way against the resistances lying in his organization, to which pain necessarily also belongs.

Whoever strives after ideals of noble greatness does so because they are the content of his being, and realizing them will be an enjoyment for him compared to which the pleasure that pettiness draws from satisfying commonplace drives is trifling. Idealists *revel*, spiritually, in translating their ideals into reality.

Whoever wants to eradicate the pleasure of satisfying human desires must first make the human being into a slave who does not act because he wants to, but only because he ought. For, the attainment of what he wants gives pleasure. What one calls *the good* is not that which the human being *ought*, but rather that which he *wants*, when he unfolds his full true human nature. Whoever does not acknowledge this must first drive out of man what he wants, and then let be prescribed for him *from outside* what he has to give as content to his willing.

Man attaches value to the fulfillment of a desire, because the desire springs from his being. What is attained has value because it is wanted. If one denies any value to the goal of human willing as such, then one must take the goals that do have value from something that a person does not want.

The ethics which builds upon pessimism springs from a disregard of moral imagination. Only one who does not consider the individual human spirit capable of giving to itself the content of its striving can seek the sum total of all willing in the longing for pleasure. The unimaginative person creates no moral ideas. They must be given to him. Physical nature provides for his striving after satisfaction of his lower desires. But to the unfolding of the *whole* human being there belong also the desires originating out of the spirit. Only when one is of the opinion that man simply does not have these, can one maintain that he must receive them from outside. Then one is also justified in saying that he is obligated to do something which he does not want. Every ethics which demands of the human being that he suppress his wanting in order to fulfill tasks which he does not want, does not reckon with the *whole* human being, but rather with one who lacks the ability to desire spiritually. For the harmoniously developed human being the so-called ideas of the good are not *outside*, but rather *inside*, the circle of his being. Moral action does not lie in the extermination of a one-sided self-will, but rather in the *full* development of human nature. Whoever regards moral ideas as attainable only if the human being extinguishes his self-will does not know that these ideals are just as much wanted by the human being as is the satisfaction of his so-called animalistic drives.

There is no denying that the views thus characterized can easily be misunderstood. Immature people without moral imagination like to regard the instincts of their half-developed nature as the full content of humanity, and they reject all moral ideas not created by them so that they can "express themselves" undisturbed. It is obvious that what is right for a whole human being is not valid for a partially developed human nature. Someone who must still first be brought by education to the point that his moral nature breaks through the shell of his lower passions: of him one cannot expect what does, however, hold good for the mature human being. But the intention here is not to delineate what needs to be instilled into the undeveloped man, but rather what lies in the nature of a fully mature human being. For the intention is to show the possibility of being free; inner freedom, however, does not appear in actions performed out of sensory or soul constraints, but rather in such actions as are carried by spiritual intuitions.

This fully mature human being gives himself his own worth. It is not pleasure he seeks, handed to him by nature or by his creator as a gift of grace; nor is it some abstract duty that he fulfills, recognized by him as such after he has stripped away all striving for pleasure. He acts as he wants, that is, in accordance with his moral intuitions; and he experiences the attainment of what he wants as his true enjoyment in life. He determines the value of life by the relation of what he has attained to what he has striven to achieve. An ethics that puts, in the place of what one wants, what one merely ought, and in the place of inclination mere duty, determines the value of man by the relation of what duty demands to what he fulfills. Such an ethics measures man by a yardstick applied from outside his being.—The view developed in this book refers man back to himself. It recognizes as the true value of life only that which the individual person regards as such in accordance with his own willing. It knows just as little about any value of life not recognized by the individual as it does about any purpose of life not springing from the individual himself. It sees in the real individual, looked upon and through from all sides, his own master and his own evaluator.

Addendum to the Revised Edition of 1918. One can misconstrue what is presented in this chapter if one gets one's teeth too firmly into the seeming objection that man's willing as such is in fact irrational, that one must show him this irrationality; then he will recognize that the goal of moral striving must lie in final liberation from willing. This kind of a seeming objection was offered me, in any case, by a competent person, who said to me that it is in fact the task of philosophy to make up for what the thoughtlessness of the animals and of most people has neglected to do; namely, to draw up a real balance sheet of life. Still, whoever makes this objection does not in fact see the main point: If inner freedom is to realize itself, then within human nature willing must be carried by intuitive thinking; but at the same time, it is a fact that willing can also be determined by something other than intuition, yet *only* in the free realizing, flowing from man's being, of intuition do there arise what is moral and the value of what is moral. Ethical individualism is able to present morality in its full worthiness, for it does not view *that* as truly moral which brings about, in an outer way, a congruence of human willing with some norm, but rather *that* which arises out of man when he unfolds moral willing as one part of his total being, in such a way that to do what is immoral seems to him as mutilation and deformation of his being.

XIV
Individuality and Genus

Against the view that the human being has it in him to
be a complete, self-contained, free individuality, there
seems to stand the fact that he appears as a part within a
natural whole (race, ancestral line, folk, family, male or
female gender), and that he is active within a whole (state,
church, and so on). He bears the general characteristics
of the community to which he belongs, and gives a content to his actions which is determined by the place he
holds within the larger group.

Given this, is individuality still possible at all? Can
one still regard the human being himself as whole in himself, seeing that he grows out of one whole and integrates
himself into another?

A part of a whole, in its characteristics and functions,
is determined by the whole. An ethnic group is a whole,
and everyone belonging to it bears the characteristic traits
that are determined by the nature of the group. How the
single person is constituted and how he acts is determined
by the character of the group. Through this the physiog-
nomy and behavior of the individual person takes on

something of a generic quality. If we ask for the reason why this or that about a person is this or that way, then we are directed away from the individual person and toward his genus. The genus explains to us why something about him appears in the form in which we observe it.

The human being frees himself, however, from these generic qualities. For man's generic qualities, when rightly experienced by him, are not something which restrict his freedom, and should also not be made to do so by artificial means. The human being develops traits and functions for himself whose determining factors can only be sought within man himself. His generic qualities serve him thereby only as a medium through which to express his particular being. He uses the characteristic traits given by nature as a basis and gives to what is generic a form in accordance with his own being. Now we would seek in vain the reason for an action of this being within the laws of the genus. We have to do with an individual who can be explained only through himself. If a person has won his way through to this detachment from the generic, and if, even then, we still want to explain everything about him by the characteristics of the genus, then we have no organ for what is individual.

It is impossible to understand a person entirely, if one bases one's judgment upon a generic concept. One persists the most in judging according to the genus where it is a matter of gender. A man sees in a woman, a woman in a man, almost always too much of the general characteristics of the opposite sex and too little of what is individual. In practical life this does less harm to men than to women. The social position of women is such an unworthy one mostly because in many respects what her position ought to be is not determined by the individual qualities of a particular woman but rather by the general picture one forms of the natural task and the needs of women. The activities of a man direct themselves in life according to his individual abilities and inclinations; those of a woman are supposed to be determined exclusively through the fact that she is after all a woman. A woman is supposed to be a slave to what is generic, to womanhood in general. As long as it is debated by men whether a woman is fitted "by natural disposition" for this or that profession, the so-called woman's question cannot get out of its most elementary stage. What a woman can want according to her nature must be left up to the woman to judge. If it is true that women are fitted only to the tasks which are presently theirs, then they will hardly be able out of themselves to attain to any others. But they must be allowed to determine for themselves what is in accordance with their nature. The response to someone who fears an upheaval of our social structure if women are to be regarded, not as generic entities, but rather as individuals, is that a social structure in which one half of mankind leads an existence unworthy of a human being is in fact very much in need of improvement.*

*Immediately upon publication of this book (1894) the objection was raised against the above arguments, that, within her generic sphere a woman can already now live out her life just as individualistically as she could want, much more freely than a man can, who, through schooling and then through war and profession is already stripped of his individuality. I know that one will raise this objection perhaps even more strongly today. In spite of this I must still let these

Whoever judges people according to generic characteristics gets only as far, in fact, as the boundary line beyond
which people start to become beings whose activity is based
upon free self-determination. What lies below this boundary can, of course, be the object of scientific study. The
characteristic traits of races, ancestral lines, peoples, and
sexes are the content of particular sciences. Only people
who wanted to live solely as examples of a genus, could
make themselves coincide with the general image which
arises out of the observations of such sciences. All these
sciences, however, cannot penetrate through to the particular content of the individual. Where the realm of
freedom (of thinking and doing) begins, the determining
of the individual by generic laws ends. The conceptual
content which man, through his thinking, must bring into
connection with perception in order to take hold of full
reality (see page 77ff.), this no one can establish once and
for all and leave behind for mankind in a finished form.
Each individual must gain his concepts through his own
intuition. How the individual person is to think cannot
be deduced from any generic concepts. It is purely and
simply the individual who decides this. And just as little
should the concrete goals which the individual wants to
set for his willing be determined out of general human
characteristics. Whoever wants to understand the single
individuality must enter into his particular being, and not

---

sentences stand here and would like to hope that there will also be
readers who understand how great a violence such an objection does
to the concept of inner freedom which is developed in this book, and
who will judge the above sentences of mine by something other than by
how a man is stripped of his individuality by schooling and profession.

stop short at typical characteristics. In this sense every single human being is a riddle. And every science that concerns itself with abstract thoughts and generic concepts is only a preparation for that knowledge which is afforded us when a human individuality communicates to us his way of viewing the world, and for that other knowledge which we gain from the content of his willing. Wherever we have the feeling that here we have to do with that in a person which is free of any typical way of thinking and free of any generic willing, there we must cease from taking recourse to any concept out of our spirit, if we want to understand his being. The activity of knowing consists in the joining of concept and perception through thinking. With all other objects the observer must gain his concepts through his intuition; with understanding a free individuality it is only a matter of purely (without mixing in our own conceptual content) taking over into our spirit his concepts, by which he, after all, determines himself. People who immediately mix their own concepts into every judgment about another person can never arrive at an understanding of an individuality. Just as the free individuality makes himself free of the characteristics of the genus, so must our knowing activity free itself from the way generic qualities are understood.

Only to the extent that a person has made himself free of generic qualities in the way indicated does he come into consideration as a free spirit within a human community. No man is entirely genus; none is all individuality. But every person gradually frees a greater or lesser sphere of his being, both from the generic qualities of animal life and from the commandments, ruling him, of human authorities.

In that part of his being in which he cannot attain such inner freedom, however, man is incorporated into the organism of nature and of the spirit. He lives in this respect as he sees others live, or as they command. Only that part of his actions which springs from his intuitions has an ethical value in the true sense. And whatever he has about him in the way of moral instincts, inherited from social instincts, becomes something ethical through his taking it up into his intuitions. All moral activity of mankind springs from individual ethical intuitions and from their being taken up into human communities. One can also say that the moral life of mankind is the sum total of the creations of the moral imagination of free human individuals. These are the findings of monism.

FINAL QUESTIONS

The Consequences of Monism

The explanation of the world as a unity, or what is meant here by monism, takes from human experience the principles it needs to explain the world. It likewise seeks the sources of man's actions within the world of observation, namely within the human nature accessible to our self-knowledge, and more particularly within moral imagination. Monism refuses to seek *outside* of this world, through abstract inferences, the ultimate foundations of the world which is present to perception and thinking. For monism, the unity which experienceable thinking observation brings to the varied multiplicity of perceptions is at the same time the unity which our human need for knowledge demands; and this need seeks entry into the physical and spiritual realms of the world through this unity. Whoever seeks, behind the unity sought in this way, yet another one only shows that he does not recognize the harmony which exists between what is found through thinking and what is demanded by our drive for knowledge. The single human individual is not really separated off from the world. He is a part of the world, and there exists in reality a connection—between this part and the totality of the cosmos—which is broken only for our perception. We see this part at first as a self-existent being, because we do not see the belts by which the fundamental powers of the cosmos turn the wheel of our life. Whoever remains at this standpoint regards a part of the whole as a being that really exists independently, regards it as the monad which receives information about the rest of the world in some way or other from outside. What is meant here by monism shows that this independence can be believed in only as long as what is perceived is not woven by thinking into the web of the conceptual world. If this is done, then this partial existence turns out to be a mere *illusion of perception*. Man can find his self-contained total existence in the universe only through the intuitive experience of thinking. Thinking destroys the illusion of perception and members our individual existence into the life of the cosmos. The unity of the conceptual world, which contains our objective perceptions, also takes up the content of our subjective personality into itself. Thinking gives us reality in its true form, as a self-contained unity, whereas the multiplicity of our perceptions is only an illusion due to our organization (see page 76ff.). The knowledge of what is real in contrast to what is illusion about perception has constituted in all ages the goal of thinking. Science has made great efforts to know perceptions as reality by discovering the lawful relationships among them. Where one was of the view, however, that the relationship ascertained by human thinking has only a subjective significance, one sought the true ground of unity in some object lying beyond our world of experience (an inferred God, will, absolute spirit, etc.).—And, based on this belief, one strove to gain, in addition to knowledge about the relationships recognizable within our experience, yet a second knowledge which goes beyond our experience, and which reveals the relationship of experience to entities that are no longer experienceable (a metaphysics attained not through experience, but rather through deduction). The reason we can grasp world relationships through orderly thinking was seen from this standpoint to lie in the fact that a primal being had built the world according to logical laws, and the reason we act was seen to lie in the willing of the primal being. But one did not recognize that thinking encompasses both what is subjective and what is objective, and that in the union of perception and concept total reality is conveyed. Only so long as we look at the lawfulness permeating and determining our perceptions, in the abstract form of the concept, do we in fact have to do with something purely subjective. But the content of the concept, which with the help of thinking is gained in addition to the perception, is not subjective. This content is not taken from the subject, but rather from reality. It is that part of reality which perceiving cannot attain. It is experience, but not experience conveyed through perception. Whoever cannot picture to himself that the concept is something real, thinks only of the abstract form in which he holds the concept in his mind. But in such a separated state the concept is present only through our organization, in the same way that the perception is. Even the tree that one perceives has, isolated off by itself, no existence. It is only a part within the great mechanism of nature, and only possible in real connection with it. An abstract concept is by itself no more real than a perception by itself. The perception is the part of reality that is given objectively; the concept is the part given subjectively (through intuition, see page 84ff.). Our spiritual organization tears reality apart into these two factors. The one factor appears to perception, the other to intuition. Only the union of both, the perception incorporating itself lawfully into the universe, is full reality. If we look at mere perception by itself, we then have no reality, but rather a disconnected chaos; if we look at the lawfulness of our perceptions by itself, we then have to do merely with abstract concepts. The abstract concept does not contain reality; but the thinking observation does indeed do so, which considers neither concept nor perception one-sidedly by itself, but rather the union of both.

That we live within reality (that the roots of our real existence extend down into reality), this even the most orthodox subjective idealist will not deny. He will only dispute the claim that we also reach ideally, with our knowing activity, into that which we really live through. With respect to this, monism shows that thinking is neither subjective nor objective, but rather a principle encompassing both sides of reality. When we observe and think, we carry out a process which itself belongs in the course of real happening. Through thinking, within the very realm of experience itself, we overcome the one-sidedness of mere perceiving. We cannot figure out the nature of what is real through abstract conceptual hypotheses (through purely conceptual thinking), but inasmuch as we find in addition to perceptions their ideas, we *live* within what is real. Monism does not seek, in addition to experience, anything unexperienceable (in the beyond), but rather sees in concept and perception what is real. It spins out of mere abstract concepts no metaphysics, because it sees in the concept by itself only the *one* side of reality which remains hidden to perception and has significance only in connection with perception. Monism calls forth within man the conviction, however, that he lives in the world of reality and does not have to seek outside his world some unexperienceable higher reality. He refrains from seeking the absolutely real anywhere other than in experience, because he recognizes the content of experience itself as the real. And he is satisfied with this reality, because he knows that thinking has the power to guarantee it. What dualism first seeks behind behind the world of observation, monism finds within this world itself. Monism shows that in our knowing activity we grasp reality in its true form, not in a subjective picture that, as it were, inserts itself between man and reality. For monism the conceptual content of the world is the same for all human individuals (see page 78ff.). According to monistic principles one human individual regards another as a being of his own kind because it is the same world content which expresses itself in him. In the oneness of the world of concepts there are not, so to speak, as many concepts "lion" as there are individual people who think "lion," but rather only *one* concept. And the concept which A adds to his perception of the lion is the same as that of B, only grasped by a different perceiving subject (see pages 79–80). Thinking leads all perceiving subjects to the common ideal oneness of all manifoldness. The oneness of the world of ideas expresses itself in them as in a multiplicity of individuals. As long as a person grasps himself merely through self-perception, he regards himself as this particular person; as soon as he looks toward the world of ideas lighting up in him and encompassing all particulars, he sees the absolutely real light up livingly within him. Dualism designates the divine primal being as that which permeates all men and lives in them all. Monism finds this universal divine life within reality itself. The ideal content of another person is also my own, and I see it as a different one only so long as I perceive; but no longer, however, as soon as I think. Every person encompasses with his thinking only a part of the total world of ideas, and to this extent individuals do also differ in the actual content of their thinking. But these contents exist in one self-contained whole which comprises the contents of thinking of all men. In his thinking, therefore, man grasps the universal primal being that permeates all men. Filled with the content of thought, his life within reality is at the same time life in God. The merely inferred unexperienceable "beyond" rests on the misunderstanding of those who believe that the "here" does not have the basis of its existence within itself. They do not recognize that through thinking they do find what they require as explanation for perception. Therefore no speculation has ever yet brought to light any content that has not been borrowed from the reality given us. The God assumed by abstract deduction is only the human being transferred into the beyond; the Will of Schopenhauer is only the human power of will made into an absolute; Hartmann's unconscious, primordial being, composed of idea and will, is a composition of two abstractions taken from experience. Exactly the same is to be said of all other principles, not based on experienceable thinking, of some "beyond."

The human spirit, in truth, never passes out of or beyond the reality in which we live, and it is also not necessary for it to do so, since everything it needs to explain the world lies within this world. If philosophers finally declare themselves satisfied with their derivation of the world out of principles which they borrow from experience and transfer into some hypothetical "beyond," then a similar satisfaction must also be possible when the same content is left in the "here" where, for experienceable thinking, it belongs. All going out of and beyond the world is only a seeming one, and principles transferred outside the world do not explain the world better than the principles lying within it. But thinking which understands itself also does not at all demand any such transcendence, since a thought content can only seek inside the world, not outside of it, for the perceptible content along with which it forms something real. Even the objects of imagination are only contents which first have validity when they become mental pictures which refer to some content of perception. Through this content of perception they incorporate themselves into reality. A concept which is supposed to be filled with a content that supposedly lies outside the world given us is an abstraction which corresponds to no reality. We can only think up the *concepts* of reality; in order to find reality itself, perceiving is also still necessary. A primal being of the world, for which a content is *thought up*, is, for a thinking which understands itself, an impossible assumption. Monism does not deny what is ideal; it in fact does not regard a content of perception which lacks its ideal counterpart as full reality; but it finds nothing in the whole domain of thinking which could make it necessary to step out of thinking's realm of experience by denying the objective spiritual reality of thinking. Monism sees, in a science which restricts itself to describing perceptions without pressing forward to their ideal complements, a half of something. But it regards in the same way, as half of something, all abstract concepts which do not find their complement in perception and do not fit in anywhere into the web of concepts that encompasses the observable world. Monism knows therefore no ideas which point toward something objective lying beyond our experience, and which supposedly form the content of a merely hypothetical metaphysics. Everything which mankind has brought forth in the form of such ideas is for monism an abstraction from experience whose creators overlook its source.

Just as little, by monistic principles, can the goals of our actions be taken from some "beyond" outside man. Insofar as they are thought, they must stem from human intuition. Man does not make the purposes of some objective primal being (in the beyond) into his individual purposes, but rather pursues purposes of his own, given him by his moral imagination. The human being looses from the one world of ideas the idea which is to be realized through some action, and lays it as the basis for his willing. In his actions, therefore, it is not the commandments instilled from the "beyond" into the "here" which express themselves, but rather human intuitions belonging to the world of the "here." Monism knows no world director who sets the goals and direction of our actions from outside of ourselves. Man finds no kind of primal ground of existence in the beyond whose decrees he could discover in order to experience from it the goals toward which he has to steer in his actions. He is thrown back upon himself. He himself must give a content to his actions. When he seeks outside of the world in which he lives for determining factors of his willing, he then searches in vain. He must seek them—when he goes beyond the satisfying of his natural drives, for which mother nature has provided—within his own moral imagination, unless his desire for comfort prefers to let itself be determined by the moral imagination of others; that means he must give up all action or else act according to determining factors which he gives himself out of the world of his ideas, or which others give him out of that same world. Whenever he goes beyond living in his sensual drives and beyond carrying out the orders of other people, he is determined by nothing other than himself. He must act out of an impulse which he has given himself and which is determined by nothing else. Ideally this impulse is, to be sure, determined within the one world of ideas; but factually it can only be drawn out of that world by man and transferred into reality. Only within man himself can monism find the basis for the actual transferring of an idea into reality by man. In order for an idea to become an action, man first must *want and will* before it can happen. This kind of willing has its basis therefore only within man himself. Man is then the one ultimately determining his action. He is *free*.

First Addendum to the Revised Edition of 1918. In the second part of this book the attempt was made to establish the fact that inner freedom is to be found in the real-

ity of human action. For this it was necessary to isolate
from the total domain of human actions those parts with
respect to which, out of unprejudiced self-observation,
one can speak of inner freedom. It is those actions which
present themselves as realizations of ideal intuitions. No
unprejudiced consideration will regard other actions as
free. But, out of unprejudiced self-observation, man will
indeed have to regard himself as able and inclined to advance upon the road to ethical intuitions and to their
realization. *This* unprejudiced observation of the ethical
being of man cannot by itself, however, establish any
final judgment about inner freedom. For were intuitive
thinking itself to spring from some other being, were its
being not one resting upon itself, then the consciousness,
flowing from what is ethical, of inner freedom would prove
to be an illusory thing. But the second part of this book
finds its natural support in the first. This presents intuitive thinking as experienced inner spiritual activity* of
man. To understand, to *experience, this* being of thinking,
however, is equivalent to knowledge of the *freedom* of intuitive thinking. And if one knows that this thinking is
free, then one also sees the perimeter of the willing to
which freedom must be ascribed. The acting human being
will be regarded as *free* by anyone who, on the basis of
inner experience, can ascribe to the intuitive thought experience its self-sustained being. Whoever is not able to
do so will definitely not be able to find any indisputable
way to the acceptance of inner freedom. The experience
presented here finds *within consciousness* the intuitive

Geistbetätigung

thinking which does not have reality only within consciousness. And it finds therefore that freedom is the characteristic feature of actions flowing from the intuitions of consciousness.

★ ★ ★

Second Addendum to the Revised Edition of 1918. What is presented in this book is built upon purely spiritual, experienceable, intuitive thinking, through which every perception is placed knowingly into reality. The book intends to present nothing more than can be surveyed out of the experience of intuitive thinking. But the intention was also to show what thought configurations this experienced thinking requires. And it requires that thinking not be denied as a self-sustaining experience within the cognitive process. It requires that one not deny thinking its ability, together with perception, to experience reality, and that one therefore not seek reality only within a world which lies outside this experience, which is only inferable, and in the face of which human thought activity is only something subjective.

Thus in thinking the element is characterized through which the human being enters spiritually into reality. (And no one really should confuse this world view, built upon experienced thinking, with any mere rationalism). But on the other hand it is fully evident from the whole spirit of what is presented here, that the perceptual element can be considered a reality for human knowledge only when it is grasped in thinking. The characterizing of something as reality cannot lie *outside* of thinking. It should therefore not be imagined, for example, that the senses' kind of perception establishes the only reality. The human being must simply *await* what will arise as perception along his life's path. The only question could be whether, from the point of view that results purely out of intuitively experienced thinking, it can justifiably be *expected* that man would be able to *perceive*, besides what is sense-perceptible, also what is spiritual. This can be expected. For although *on the one hand* intuitively experienced thinking is an active process taking place within the human spirit, *on the other hand* it is at the same time a spiritual perception grasped without any physical organ. It is a perception in which the perceiver himself is active, and it is an activity of the self which is also perceived. In intuitively experienced thinking man is transferred into a spiritual world also as perceiver. Within this world, whatever comes to meet him as perception in the same way that the spiritual world of his own thinking does, this the human being recognizes to be the world of spiritual perception.* *This* world of perception would have the same relation to thinking which the world of physical perception does on the side of the senses. The world of spiritual perception, as soon as man experiences it, cannot be anything foreign to him, because in intuitive thinking he already has an experience that bears a purely spiritual character. A number of books published by me after this one speak about such a world of spiritual perception. This *Philosophy of Spiritual Activity* lays the philosophical groundwork for these later books. For in this book the attempt is made to show that the experience of thinking, rightly understood, *is* already the experiencing of spirit. Therefore it seems to

geistige Wahrnehmungswelt

the author that a person will not stop short before entering the world of spiritual perception who can in full earnestness take the point of view of the author of this *Philosophy of Spiritual Activity*. What is presented in the author's later books cannot, it is true, be logically drawn —by deductive reasoning—out of the content of this book. From a living grasp of what is meant in this book by intuitive thinking, however, there will quite naturally result the further living entry into the world of spiritual perception.

First Appendix
(Addendum to the Revised Edition of 1918)

Certain objections raised from philosophical quarters immediately after the appearance of this book move me to add the following brief comments to this new edition. I can very well imagine that there are readers interested in the content of this book who will nevertheless regard the following as a superfluous, remote, and abstract spinning out of concepts. They can leave this brief presentation unread. However, within the philosophical way of looking at the world, problems arise which have their origin more in certain preconceptions of thinkers than in the natural course of general human thinking. What is otherwise taken up in this book seems to me to be a task which concerns *every* person who is struggling for clarity with respect to the being of man and his relationship to the world. What follows, however, is more a problem that certain philosophers demand be taken up when the things presented in this book are discussed, because, through their way of picturing things, these philosophers have created for themselves certain difficulties not generally present. If one completely bypasses such problems, then certain personalities are quick at hand with the reproach of dilettantism and the like. And there arises an opinion as though the author of a presentation like the one given in this book had not come to terms with views which he does not discuss within the book itself.

The problem to which I refer is this: there are thinkers who are of the opinion that a particular difficulty arises when one wants to grasp how another human soul life could affect one's own (the observer's). They say that my conscious world is enclosed within me; and the other conscious world likewise within itself. I cannot see into the world of consciousness of another. How do I arrive at knowing myself to be in a common world with him? That world view which regards it as possible to infer, from the conscious world, an unconscious one that can never become conscious attempts to solve this difficulty in the following fashion. It says that the world which I have in my consciousness is a representation in me of a world of reality not consciously attainable by me. In this world of reality lie the unknown causes of my world of consciousness. In it lies also my real being, of which I likewise have only a representation in my consciousness. In it lies also, however, the being of the other person who approaches me. Now what is experienced in the consciousness of this other person has its corresponding reality, independent of his consciousness, within his being. This reality works in the realm that cannot become conscious upon my essential unconscious being, and through this a representation is created in my consciousness for that which is present in a consciousness that is completely independent of my conscious experience. One can see that here, in addition to the world accessible to my consciousness, a world is hypothetically constructed which cannot be experienced by this consciousness, because otherwise one believes oneself forced to maintain that all the outer world which I believe I have before me is only my world of consciousness, and that would result in the solipsistic absurdity that other people also live only within my consciousness.

Clarity can be gained on this question, raised by many epistemological tendencies of our day, if one undertakes to look at the matter from the point of view of observation in accordance with the spirit taken in the presentation of this book. What do I have before me then to begin with when I confront another personality? I look at what is most immediate. This is the bodily manifestation of the other person given to me as perception; then in addition perhaps the audible perception of what he says, and so on. I do not merely stare at all this, but rather it sets my thinking activity in motion. Inasmuch as I stand, thinking, before the other personality, the perception reveals to me its characteristic of being in a certain way transparent to the soul. I am obliged, in grasping the perception in thinking, to say to myself that it is not at all that which it appears to be to the outer senses. The physical manifestation reveals, within what it is directly, something else which it is indirectly. Its placing itself before me is at the same time its extinguishing as a merely physical manifestation. But what it brings to manifestation in this extinguishing compels me as a thinking being to extinguish my thinking during the time of its working and to set in the place of my thinking, *its* thinking. *Its* thinking, however, I grasp within my thinking as an experience like my own. I have really perceived the thinking of the other person. For the direct perception which extinguishes itself as a physical manifestation is grasped by my thinking, and this is an occurrence lying completely *within* my consciousness, an occurrence which consists in the fact that the other thinking takes the place of my thinking. Through the physical manifestation's extinguishing itself, the separation between the two spheres of consciousness is actually removed. This represents itself within my consciousness through the fact that, in experiencing the other content of consciousness, I experience my own consciousness just as little as I experience it in dreamless sleep. Just as in dreamless sleep my day consciousness is excluded, so in perceiving the other content of consciousness my own content is excluded. What keeps me from recognizing this is only the fact that, firstly, when I perceive the other person, unconsciousness does not enter the place where the content of my own consciousness is extinguished as in sleep, but rather the other content of consciousness enters, and secondly, that the alternating states of the extinguishing and lighting up again of my consciousness of myself succeed one another too quickly to be usually noticed.—The whole problem lying before us here is not to be solved by artificial constructs of concepts which infer something conscious-in-itself that can never become conscious, but rather by true experiencing of what results from the joining of thinking and perception. This is the case with very many of the questions which appear in philosophical literature. Thinkers should seek the way to unprejudiced observation in accordance with the spirit; instead of this they thrust an artificial construct of concepts in front of reality.

In an essay by Eduard von Hartmann on "The Ultimate Questions of Epistemology and Metaphysics" (in the Journal of Philosophy and Philosophical Criticism, Vol. 108, p. 55ff.)* my *Philosophy of Spiritual Activity* is included in that philosophical direction of thought which wishes to base itself upon an "epistemological monism." Such a standpoint is rejected by Eduard von Hartmann as an impossible one. He does this for the following reasons. According to the way of picturing things brought to expression in his essay, there are only three possible epistemological standpoints. Either a person remains at the naive standpoint, which takes the manifestations it perceives to be real things outside of human consciousness. Then one would lack critical knowledge. One would not see that one is, with one's content of consciousness, still only within one's own consciousness. One would not recognize that one does not have to do with a "table-in-itself," but rather only with an object of one's own consciousness. Whoever remains at this standpoint or returns to it again through some consideration or other, is a naive realist. But this standpoint is impossible, however, for it overlooks the fact that consciousness has only its own objects of consciousness. Or one recognizes this state of affairs and admits it to oneself fully. Then one becomes at first a transcendental idealist. But then one would have to reject the possibility that anything of a "thing-in-itself" could ever appear within human consciousness. Through this, however, one cannot escape absolute illusionism, if one is only consistent enough about it. For the world

---

*"*Die letzten Fragen der Erkenntnistheorie und Metaphysik,*" *Zeitschrift für Philosophie und philosophische Kritik.*

which one confronts transforms itself for one into a mere
sum total of objects of consciousness, and in fact only of
objects of one's own consciousness. One is then compelled
—and this is absurd—to think that even other people as
objects are present only in one's own content of consciousness alone. Only the third standpoint, transcendental
realism, is a possible one. It assumes that there are
"things-in-themselves," but that consciousness cannot
in any way have anything to do with them in immediate
experience. Beyond human consciousness, in a way that
does not enter consciousness, they bring it about that
within consciousness the objects of consciousness appear.
One can come to these "things-in-themselves" only
through inferences drawn from the content of one's consciousness which alone is experienced but which in fact is
merely one's mental pictures. Now Eduard von Hartmann
maintains, in the essay mentioned above, that an "epistemological monism," which he considers my standpoint
to be, would have to espouse one of the three standpoints; it does not do so only because it does not draw the
actual conclusions lying within its presuppositions. And
then in the essay it is said, "If one wants to find out to
which epistemological standpoint a supposed epistemological monist belongs, then one needs only to lay a few
questions before him and to compel him to answer them.
For of himself no such monist will ever venture any ut-
terance on these points, and he will even seek in every
way to evade answering direct questions, because every
answer invalidates the claim of epistemological monism
as to its being a different standpoint than the other three.
These questions are the following: 1. Are things *con-*

tinuous or *intermittent* in their existence? If the answer is that they are continuous, then one has to do with naive realism in one form or another. If the answer is that they are intermittent, then it is a case of transcendental idealism. But if the answer is that they are on the one hand (as content of the absolute consciousness, or as unconscious mental pictures or as perceptual possibilities) continuous, and on the other hand (as content of our limited consciousness) intermittent, then transcendental realism is established. 2. If three people are sitting at a table, *how many specimens of the table* are present? Whoever answers 'one,' is a naive realist; whoever answers 'three' is a transcendental idealist; but whoever answers 'four,' he is a transcendental realist. It is, to be sure, assumed in this, that one is allowed to draw together into one common appelation 'specimens of the table,' such unlike things as the table as thing-in-itself, and the three tables as objects of perception within the three consciousnesses. If this seems too great a liberty to anyone, he will have to give the answer 'one and three' instead of 'four.' 3. If two people are alone together in a room, *how many specimens of these people* are present? Whoever answers 'two' is a naive realist; whoever answers 'four' (namely, in each of the two consciousnesses, one ego and one other), he is a transcendental idealist; but whoever answers 'six' (namely, two people as things-in-themselves, and four mental pictures of people within the two consciousnesses), he is a transcendental realist. Whoever wanted to show that epistemological monism is a different standpoint than these three, would have to give to each of these three questions some different answer; I wouldn't know, however, what they could be.'' The answers of the *Philosophy of Spiritual Activity* would have to be: 1. Whoever grasps only the perceptual content of things and considers this to be reality is a naive realist, and he does not make it clear to himself that he should actually regard *this perceptual content* as existing only for as long as he is looking at the things, that therefore he would have to think of what he has before him as intermittent. As soon as he becomes clear about the fact, however, that reality is present only when the perceptible is permeated with thought, will he attain the insight that the content of perception, appearing as intermittent, if permeated by what is worked out in thinking, reveals itself to be continuous. We must therefore regard as continuous the perceptual content grasped by a thinking which is experienced; the part of this content that is only perceived would have to be thought of as intermittent, if —which is not the case—it were real.—2. If three people are sitting at a table, how many specimens of the table are present? There is only *one* table present; but *as long as* the three people wanted to stop short at their perceptual pictures, they would have to say that *these* perceptual pictures are definitely no reality. As soon as they proceed to the table grasped in their thinking, the *one* reality of the table reveals itself to them; they are united with their three contents of consciousness within this reality.—3. If two people are alone together in a room, how many specimens of these people are present? There are quite certainly not six—not even in the sense of the transcendental realist—specimens present, but only two. Only, each of the persons has at first, both of himself and of the other person, only his unreal perceptual picture. Of these *pictures* there are four present, through whose presence within the thinking activities of the two persons the grasping of reality takes place. In this thinking activity each of the persons reaches beyond his sphere of consciousness; the sphere of consciousness, the other person's and his own, comes to life in this activity. In the moment this comes to life the two people are enclosed just as little within their consciousness as they are in sleep. But in the other moments, the consciousness of this merging with the other consciousness arises again, in such a way that, in thinking experience the consciousness of each one of the two people grasps himself and the other. I know that the transcendental realist will call this a relapse into naive realism. However, I have already indicated in this book that naive realism still holds good for thinking which is experienced. The transcendental realist does not enter at all into the true state of affairs with respect to the cognitive process; he closes himself off from this through a web of thoughts and entangles himself in it. The monism which appears in *The Philosophy of Spiritual Activity* should also not be called "epistemological," but rather, if one wishes a second name, thought-monism. All this was misunderstood by Eduard von Hartmann. He did not enter into that which is particular in what *The Philosophy of Spiritual Activity* presents, but rather asserted that I had made the attempt to combine Hegel's universalistic panlogism with Hume's individualistic phenomenalism (p. 71 of the Journal of Philosophy, Vol. 108, footnote),★

★*Zeitschrift fur Philosophie*

whereas in fact *The Philosophy of Spiritual Activity* as such has absolutely nothing to do with these two standpoints which it is supposedly trying to unite. (This is also the reason I could not be concerned about coming to terms, for example, with the "epistemological monism" of Johannes Rehmke. The point of view of *The Philosophy of Spiritual Activity* is, in fact, completely different from what Eduard von Hartmann and others call epistemological monism.)

Second Appendix

In the following there is given again, in all its essential points, what stood as a kind of preface to the first edition of this book. Since it gives more the mood of thought out of which I wrote the book twenty-five years ago than the book's content, I bring it here as an "appendix." I do not want to leave it out entirely, for the reason that the view always comes up again that because of my later spiritual–scientific writings I have something to suppress in my earlier writings.

Our age can wish to draw the *truth* only out of the depths of man's being.* Of Schiller's well-known two ways, the second will especially benefit the present day:

> Truth we both are seeking, you in the life without,
> I within the heart, and so each finds it surely.
> Is the eye healthy, it meets the creator without;
> Is the heart so, it surely mirrors the world within.

*Entirely left out here are only the very first introductory sentences (of the first edition) of these considerations which seem to me today completely unessential. But the rest of what is said seems to me necessary, even now, in spite of the scientific mode of thought of our contemporaries, nay precisely because of it.

A truth which comes to us from outside always bears the stamp of uncertainty about it. What appears to each one of us within his own inner life as truth, in this only do we want to believe.

Only the truth can bring us certainty in the developing of our individual powers. Whoever is tormented by doubts, his powers are lamed. In a world which is a riddle to him, he can find no goal for his activity.

We no longer want merely to *believe*; we want *to know*. Faith demands the acceptance of truths about which we do not have full insight. That about which we do not have full insight, however, goes against what is individual, which wants to experience everything with its deepest inner life. Only that *knowing* satisfies us which submits to no outer norm, but rather springs from the inner life of the personality.

We also do not want any kind of knowing that has become frozen once and for all into rigid academic formulations and preserved in compendia valid for all time. We consider ourselves, each one, justified in taking our starting point from our immediate experiences, from what we live through directly, and in ascending from there to knowledge of the whole universe. We are striving for a sure knowing, but each in his own way.

Our scientific teachings should also no longer be formulated as though we were unconditionally compelled to accept them. No one would want to give a scientific work a title like Fichte once did: "A Crystal-clear Report to the Wider Public on the Actual Nature of the Newest Philosophy. *An Attempt to Compel Readers to Understand.*" Today, no one should be *compelled* to understand. If no definite individual need moves a person toward a certain view, we demand neither that he recognize nor agree with it. Today we do not want to funnel knowledge even into the still immature human being, the child, but rather we seek to develop his capacities, so that he no longer needs to be *compelled* to understand, but rather *wants* to understand.

I am under no illusions with respect to this characteristic of my times. I know how alive and extensive the tendency is to be stereotyped and without individuality. But I know just as well that many of my contemporaries are seeking to conduct their life in the sense and direction I have indicated. I would like to dedicate this book to them. It is not meant to be "the only possible" way to the truth, but it is meant to tell of that way which one person has taken, whose concern is for the truth.

This book leads at first into more abstract regions, where thought must draw sharp outlines in order to reach sure points. But the reader will be led out of these dry concepts into concrete life also. I am altogether of the view that one must lift oneself also into the ethereal realm of concepts, if one wants to experience existence in all directions. Whoever knows only how to enjoy with his senses does not know the real delicacies of life. Oriental sages make their pupils lead lives of renunciation and asceticism for years before they communicate what they themselves know. The West no longer demands for science any devout exercises or asceticism, but it does require, instead of these, the good will to withdraw oneself for a short time from the immediate impressions of life, and to betake oneself into the realm of the world of pure thought.

The realms of life are many. For each of these, particular sciences evolve. But life itself is a unity, and the more the sciences strive to deepen themselves in the individual realms, the more they distance themselves from a view of the living wholeness of the world. There must be a knowledge which seeks within the individual sciences the elements needed to lead man back again into full life. The scientific researcher in a particular field wants to acquire through his knowledge a consciousness of the world and its workings; in this book the goal is a philosophical one: the science itself is meant to become organically living. The individual sciences are preparatory stages of the science striven for here. A similar relationship holds sway in the arts. The composer works on the basis of the theory of composition. This last is a sum of knowledge whose acquirement is a necessary prerequisite for composing music. In composing, the laws of composition serve life, serve actual reality. In exactly the same sense philosophy is an *art*. All real philosophers were *artists in concepts*. For them human ideas became the artistic medium and the scientific method became the artistic technique. Abstract thinking thereby gains concrete individual life. Ideas become powers of life. We have then not merely a knowing about things, but rather we have made knowing into a real self-governing organism; our actual active consciousness has lifted itself above a merely passive taking up of truths.

How philosophy as an art relates itself to the *inner freedom* of man, what inner freedom is, and whether we partake in it or can become partakers in it: that is the main question of my book. All other scientific discussions are included here only because they ultimately shed light on those questions which, in my view, concern the human being most immediately. A *Philosophy of Spiritual Activity (Freiheit)* is meant to be given in these pages.

All science would only be the satisfying of idle curiosity, if it did not strive toward raising the *value of existence of the human personality.* The sciences first acquire their true value through presenting the human significance of their results. The ennobling of one single soul faculty cannot be the end purpose of the individual, but rather the development of all the abilities that slumber within us. Knowledge has value only through the fact that it contributes to the *all-around* unfolding of the *whole* nature of man.

This book does not therefore consider the relationship between science and life to be such that man has to bow down to the idea and dedicate his forces to its service, but rather in the sense that man takes possession of the world of ideas in order to use them for his *human* goals which transcend merely scientific ones.

One must be able to confront the idea, experiencing it; *otherwise* one falls into bondage to it.

Translator's Appendix

The goal of this translation is to give the reader an experience as close as possible to that presented by the original book. Rudolf Steiner, in fact, made every possible effort to write his books "in such a way that they can be translated into the other languages." (January 5, 1922; GA 303) His writing is archetypal in its expression of living ideas and lends itself readily to English. I have therefore tried to keep to his own images, pace, and style, and to his own organization of the whole into chapters, paragraphs, and sentences. I have retained one form of punctuation no longer customary in English: the use of a dash after a period to indicate subparagraphs within paragraphs. Longer quotations are left as an integral part of the text, unindented, as in the original.

This book speaks to the direct experience of any reader willing to think actively about what he observes within and around himself. No specialized background is needed. I have therefore added no annotations that might draw the reader away from the primary activity of working with Rudolf Steiner's text itself. His quotations from the

work of other thinkers are there mainly to embody particular ideas with which a free spirit must come to terms.
His book, *Riddles of Philosophy*, is recommended to anyone interested in the place these thinkers hold within the
wider context of the history of ideas.

Something must still be said about the word *Freiheit*
(literally, "freehood"). In a lecture in Dornach on January 5, 1922 (GA 303), Rudolf Steiner said of his book *Die
Philosophie der Freiheit* that it should "never bear the title
in English of 'Philosophy of Freedom.' " In a lecture in
Oxford on August 29, 1922 (GA 305), he again indicated
that *Freiheit* has a different meaning than "freedom"
does, and that in England one must speak of a "world
view of spiritual activity (*spirituelle Aktivität*)"—a world
view "of action, thinking, and feeling out of the spiritual
individuality of man." In the text, I have translated *Freiheit* as "inner freedom" (for Rudolf Steiner, Frei*heit*
points more to man's inner being than "free*dom*" does);
or as "freedom," in the case of freedom of the will, for
example.

If you are interested in other publications of the Anthroposophic Press (including over 150 titles by Rudolf Steiner) please write to:

Anthroposophic Press
RR 4, Box 94 A1
Hudson, NY 12534